Fifty of the greatest rugby league tries of all time

MARTIN OFFIAH

with Philip Spires

**View all the action from 50 Of The Best on the
book's website: www.martinoffiah.co.uk**

ISBN:978-1-905988-81-5

Cover design by Kelly Walsh

Published by Libros International

www.librosinternational.com

Printed and bound in Great Britain by
CPI Antony Rowe, Chippenham and Eastbourne

MARTIN OFFIAH

with Philip Spires

Libros
INTERNATIONAL

Acknowledgements

Thanks to:
My colleagues in Sky Sports
Stuart Evans of York Rugby League Referees Association
Mark Hebblethwaite
Ian Proctor of Sky Sports

I would like to dedicate this book to my partner and future wife Virginia Shaw, my son Tyler and my unborn child, my family.

CONTENTS

Foreword by Shaun Edwards

I first played against Martin Offiah for Wigan at Widnes in a Lancashire Cup tie. Needless to say, he scored a try, one of his trademark tries where he finished flamboyantly but effectively. We'd heard about this new try-scoring sensation and he certainly caught the eye. He'd done extremely well in his first games in rugby league and news of his speed had itself travelled fast through the game. The first time we played together, of course, was in a representative game. Martin scored a try in that game and I think it came from my pass. It was in his first season and he'd already demonstrated what rugby league could expect from him. To have continued to do it for the next ten years was exceptional.

We were friends from the start. Obviously if we played against one another we competed. But when he signed for Wigan for that world record fee, I saw a lot more of him because we were together on a day-to-day basis. It was a memorable day when he signed for Wigan. And it was not merely because of that huge fee. It was because he was the best try scorer in the world. These days I keep in touch with several of the lads I used to play with, but Martin became a true friend.

People come to watch rugby league to see tries. There are many sides to the game, of course, and they can all be exciting. There's the spectacle of a bone-crunching contact or a great cover tackle. A crowd will applaud someone who catches a high kick under pressure. But in the end the most exciting things in the game are the tries. Tries scored against strong defences are even more exciting. Often, in a high-scoring game where the defences are not perfect, the tries might not be good, because the teams don't have to work hard for them. But when you see a spectacular try scored against a good team in a big game, it's quite simply the highlight of the sport. When the defences are giving it absolutely everything, a score has to be worked for. It almost has to be constructed a piece at a time by teamwork, or sometimes it can be a great individual effort, like many of the ones that Martin scored. Great tries win games. They make the history of the sport. Tries and try-scorers are what the fans come to see. And try-scorers are often the big personalities in the game.

There are players who are known strikers, known match-winners. Many of them are happy just to be on a winning side, but there are others who want to be on the score sheet every time. Martin is in that category.

There's an opinion around that in the modern game a team can't afford a dedicated try-scorer like Martin. Strangely, the opinion is nothing new. My father, Jack, played alongside Brian Bevan at Warrington, and he told me a story that's the perfect answer to this point. There was a real character in the team at the time called Bill McFarland. Apparently someone said, "Bevan's a great player, but he doesn't tackle." Billy's answer was, "If he scores three tries every game, I'll do his tackling for him!" Billy knew where his bread was buttered. What he wanted was his winning money, and a try-scorer like Brian Bevan could secure it.

But what I will also say is that Martin underestimates the defensive side of his game. I've seen him make a host of cover tackles, and often he used his speed to cover back. I remember one particular example against Castleford in the 1992 Cup Final involving the late St John Ellis, who was a flying machine himself. He'd kicked ahead and we all thought it was a certain try because I've never seen anyone run as fast as him on a rugby field. Martin chased back, got there first and hacked the ball dead to save our bacon. And many times I've seen him put in a try-saving tackle that was only possible because he could get there!

And it's important not to lose sight of his real skill. When it comes to try scoring, and particularly in Martin's case, people always speak about speed. But I'd say there were only 25 to 30 per cent of Martin's tries where his speed was the crucial factor. More important was his speed of thought. It was when that combined with his speed of foot that he was truly lethal. And his work-rate off the ball was superb, making sure that he was always in position to make a score possible.

I didn't see some of the older players such as Boston and Bevan, but if you look at Martin's try-scoring ratio, it's as good or even better than most. Martin is certainly the equal of anyone who has ever played the game. His record proves it. He's proved it in Australia and he's proved it in test matches as well. His absolute hunger and dedication to score tries was unparalleled. There is no one in the sport more qualified to produce a book about some of its greatest scores.

Past

Welcome to my *50 Of The Best*, a personal collection of some great scores from the last thirty years of rugby league. Let's face it, rugby league is about scoring tries and I reckon I know something about that, because no other English player has scored more than I have. And it's a record that I reckon will never be bettered. But no one would be happier than me if someone did, because it would mean that the game would have been graced by a very special talent.

I retired from the game eight years ago. Since then I've done a number of things, amongst them presenting the Super League summary on Sky Sports News. During my time with Sky I've commented on hundreds of games and probably thousands of scores. I have never, however, presented my thoughts on the game in a more extended and detailed form. I've regularly reported on features of play, but only rarely described them in detail. Neither does the format of the summary offer the opportunity to pursue the stories behind the scores. My *50 Of The Best* is an opportunity to do some of these things.

The book is a collection of scores selected from the last 30 years of rugby league. It features some of the game's greatest players and some of its rookies. It describes careers that have shone and others that have turned lacklustre. Above all, it tells some of the game's compelling stories, the human aspects of the game that often are hidden under the surface. What I've tried to do is get beneath that surface.

Each piece describes a score. Of the 50 features, 49 of them describe tries. I've included seven of my own tries, while the rest are shared between 35 other players, of whom eight have two tries each. Just one piece has a different style and focus. It actually describes two tries, but neither is scored by the featured player, because his prime role in his years in the game has been largely dedicated to the role of the provider. My intention throughout my *50 Of the Best* is to describe and thus celebrate the skills and achievements of the players concerned and to uncover some of the stories behind the action. It's a book for followers of the game, but there's much the general reader will enjoy, even someone who might not be a fan of the sport, because some of the stories are simply human, interesting enough to transcend a mere technical reading.

My own career in rugby league came to an end with my retirement in 2001. I had over 14 years in the game after beginning with Widnes in 1987. The highest points of my time in the game, of course, came during my four years with Wigan. To describe the Wigan side of that era as all-conquering is, if anything, an understatement. But I was also the league's top try scorer in each of my first four seasons, and most of those were with Widnes, before I even joined the main act at Wigan.

But things move on and so did I, to London Broncos, a rugby league team outside the game's traditional heartland. It was part of an initiative to expand the base of the game, a strategy that continues to this day in the shape of Harlequins, Catalan Dragons and Celtic Crusaders.

Following rule changes in rugby union, I was able to combine my commitments to the Broncos with appearances for Bedford rugby union. I wasn't the first player to explore the newly-opened possibilities in union, but I was pretty early on the scene. Perhaps I could have achieved more in that period if I hadn't sustained injuries that kept me out of the game for significant periods. Who knows? But I was injured and the number of games I was able to play was fewer than I would have liked.

I left London Broncos in 1999. By March of that year I'd taken over third position on the list of rugby league's most prolific try-scorers. But I still had an ambition to fulfil. For me the figure of 500 tries was iconic and I was determined to reach it. Achieving that figure would still leave me third in the list and I already was number one on the list of English players. But that 500 mark would take me close enough to the career tally of the second player on the list, the legendary Billy Boston, to silence any anticipated criticism suggesting that players from earlier generations were fundamentally better.

Throughout my time in rugby league I felt that I continually had to prove myself to be taken seriously. I never really conformed to the stereotype. I was from London and I went to boarding school. I thus had no home base in the game, no comfort zone into which I could retreat if things didn't go my way. This motivated me even more to stay in control, to keep scoring tries, to put me one step ahead of the critics who I thought were always waiting for me to slip up.

Well, I made it to the 500. I also managed one more before repeated injury persuaded me to retire. It was 2001 by then and I'd played two seasons with Salford City Reds. I played a few games of union after that for Wasps, but at 35 years old I really was ready to do something different.

My career spanned three decades, the 80s, the 90s and a little of the noughties. A new decade is about to start and it almost feels as if my achievement is drifting into a history that no longer has anything to do with me. So I'm prompted to look back both on my own career and the three decades that hosted it. But now of course I look back at the game with different eyes. It's not just the perspective of the try-scorer. Now I'm interested in what led up to the score, what followed and the influence the score had on the result. There are also often consequences for the players concerned.

My viewpoint nowadays takes in not only the execution of the score, but also the detail of the player's career and the stories that surround the game itself, its prelude, its aftermath. After all, I'm now in the business of advising a number of young players about contracts, opportunities and their future development. I'm part of a process that can influence careers and, through that, achievements. Nowadays, when I see great play, I see much more than the passes, the breaks and other technicalities of the game.

When I consider where the game was in 1980 compared to where it is now in late 2009, some interesting trends and patterns emerge. During those three decades, we saw the completion of some illustrious careers. These were players of an older generation than mine. We've seen players like me, whose entire period in the game has come and gone. And now we see the emerging careers of youngsters. But what is important here is that the older group were playing rugby league when it was changing internally. The careers of players in my era straddled the transition to Super League and the change in relations with union. The younger players are seeing the game expand, both commercially and globally, and grow in a way that players of 30 years ago could not have imagined.

In 1980 most rugby league players were semi-professional. These days Super League is fully professional. In the middle of the era, in the mid-1990s, I was part of a Wigan side that was instrumental in initiating the change.

Since 1980 there's been a complete about-face in relations between the two rugby codes. I was playing when the pivotal change happened and I was one of the first professionals to mix union with league. In late 2009, this change is now taken for granted. As a consequence, the options available to young players are fundamentally different from what they were in the past.

Early in the 1980s an Australian touring team to Britain and France went home with the nickname, *Invincibles*. They'd set new standards for fitness, tactics and technique, new standards that the British game in particular couldn't match for almost a decade. During my three decades, Australia dominated the international scene, but at their end it's New Zealand who hold the World Cup. And, at the start of this era, a World Cup competition would have comprised just four teams. In 2008 more than 20 national teams entered the competition and a qualifying competition was needed to provide five of the ten finalists.

At the start of the era, British rugby league was predominantly a local, even parochial north of England sport. Towards the end of 2009, Super League is European. Its players are now drawn from a variety of countries and regularly cross codes from league to union, or vice versa, and back again!

In my *50 Of The Best* I describe scores from the game in the last 30 years that both illustrate and epitomise some of these changes. I feature players who've played a special role in my career, some of whom have assisted me, and some of whom have opposed. I've told some of the game's stories, and thrown down a gauntlet or two. There are players who have achieved almost everything the game can offer, and others whose time is surely yet to come. There are some who have achieved significant personal goals, and others who have missed out.

I've also written about three scores from before my 1980 starting point. But, as you will see, each has its own special story. One of these relates to me, another is of national significance, and the third is iconic in the history of the game.

Each score in my *50 Of The Best*, however, has its own story. Each one features a particular player who, in his own way, has achieved something special. As you'd expect, I have a soft spot for wingers and so they feature significantly in my selection. My own seven tries have their own stories as well, and they're included either because they represented high points in my career, or because they illustrate something in particular about my experience of the game.

I haven't presented the tries in any obvious order. I could have placed them chronologically, but the reason for doing so would be to identify those trends in the game that I've already mentioned. So the order is unpredictable, with links between my *50 Of The Best* often loose and idiosyncratic. Most of the scores happened on great or significant occasions, because often it's the context or the setting that renders a score truly iconic. After all, we have all scored the greatest ever try in history on the training ground! Overall, I hope the scores I have selected form a story of their own.

Throughout my selection, it's the stories that interest me. Sometimes it's a player that stands out, a remarkable life or a distinguished career, or both. Sometimes it's the setting, the history or the achievement that shines through. On occasions I can review a whole career. Sometimes the career is still in its midstream, the personal achievement as yet incomplete, its ultimate success or otherwise waiting to be assessed in another decade. I've included some of the game's greatest names and some of its lesser-knowns. Throughout, however, I want to feature the game's strengths, its spectacle and its excitement. I'm a very positive person. I don't like to dwell either on scandal or failure. Neither do I like to point fingers or to criticise. So my *50 Of The* Best is a celebration of rugby league, its players, its skills, its competitions and its settings.

But my selection, any selection, needs a theme, and so I've used a number of the game's essential qualities as a framework for my comments. Throughout, I've highlighted speed and strength, tactics and teamwork, and, finally, stealth as my yardsticks.

A rugby league player needs a combination of physical characteristics and skills. It's no good being big if you're not mobile. It's no good being fast if you can't catch the ball. It's no use having the world's most elusive sidestep if you can't work in a team. And who needs the perfect goal kicker who can't run?

So speed and strength, tactics and teamwork, spiced with stealth form my framework. The last three decades are my era. The stories associated with some great tries and other scores are my material. The players are my focus. And so I present my *50 Of The Best* as a celebration of rugby league. I can't include everything or everybody. It's just *50 Of The Best*.

The book isn't an encyclopaedia of the game. It's just my thoughts and reflections. It does, however, contain a lot of information. I've tried, of course, to ensure that everything is accurate, correct and fair. If I have made a mistake somewhere, then let me apologise here, in advance. And at the end, I've taken a sideways look at some of the current issues in the game, themes that are addressed in one way or another throughout the book.

Finally, thank you to everyone at Sky Sports for their help in preparing this book. Thank you also to the game of rugby league, the game that gave me the opportunity and the stage to live my dream.

50 Of The Best

1 – 1994

There was, of course, only ever going to be one try that would open my *50 Of The Best*. It was the very pinnacle of my career and, apart from the birth of my son, the best moment in my life. With my 1994 Wembley try scored, I was on my knees and the words that ran through my head were, "It's never going to get better than this."

'Going the length of the field' is one of those iconic phrases in rugby league. Ask any young fan of the game what forms the stuff of dreams and I'll bet that 'going the length of the field...' soon figures. The fact that it might also often be followed by '...and then diving over the crossbar to touch down!' indicates just how far into the realms of fantasy we've reached.

But it's not just young fans who dream of achieving that ultimate feat. I know many players, seasoned pros, who still allow themselves an occasional dream score. For most, it stays a dream. It's one thing for a try to go the length of the field as a result of teamwork. But when you do it all by yourself and on the greatest stage in the game, it's then that dreams turn into reality, and perhaps back again.

But often, going the length of the field comes about because of an interception. Now, interception tries are often spectacular in that the score is frequently preceded by a long sprint to the line. Paul Loughlin's 1990 try against Australia at Old Trafford comes to mind. But a successful interception usually puts you in the clear and, of course, the opposition is going the other way when you set off. The defence has to stop and turn round before the chase can start. Such tries might be spectacular, but they're rarely remembered, unless the context, like with Paul Loughlin's, is significant.

Wingers dream more about length-of-the-field tries than most. After all, it's our role to be quick and to outpace opponents. It's also our job to score tries, to exploit an overlap with pace to finish a move. In the modern game things have changed. Given the way it's played nowadays, there aren't many teams that can afford to field what I call a 'throw-back' winger, a player of the type I was, whose prime role was to attack.

And I was lucky to score many long-range tries. But I know in my heart of hearts that nothing will ever surpass the feelings that flowed through me thirteen minutes into that Challenge Cup Final of 1994.

I remember that Cup Final day feeling surreal. Looking back at it now, it seems even more so. I can remember getting up that morning and straightaway leafing through the *Daily Mirror*. Alex Murphy's column seemed to jump off the page. 'The Mouth' said I was finished and that I was only ever the best of a bad bunch. It's hard, sometimes, to imagine the distant planets where some people live!

I can remember putting the paper down and feeling

angry for a moment or two. But then I sat back and relaxed. I felt really good. I even felt confident because Wigan, and myself in particular, always seemed to do well against Leeds. But if I needed an added boost, I certainly got one from that *Mirror* piece. So, in a strange way, perhaps I owe Alex something after all, because now I had more than ability, more than confidence, more even than dreams. I had a point to prove. In retrospect, I think that winning the Lance Todd Trophy and scoring two tries, one of which was the best ever seen at Wembley, was a pretty good way of putting my side of the case.

When we went out onto the pitch I was both confident and in control but also fired up. The last time I'd felt like that I ended up scoring ten tries against Leeds in a Premiership semi-final. This time I also had something to prove and, as luck would have it, I got the opportunity I was seeking. But the game was far from straightforward. If I record that in the end we won 26-16, it sounds like little more than a continuation of the routine of Wigan's complete dominance of the competition. We'd won the Cup in the previous six seasons, a sequence that began with the win over Halifax in 1988.

But don't think for one minute that any game is easy and certainly don't even suggest that anyone ever takes success in a major competition for granted. All games have to be won and, when you walk out with a record like ours in 1994, the last thing you want, as a player, is to be part of the side that loses.

In the first ten minutes of the 1994 Final, Leeds threw everything at us, had us pinned back against our line and came close to scoring themselves. So let's join the game just after that. We're in possession near our own line, just five metres out. There are precisely 12 minutes on the clock.

We have a play-the-ball. Because we're under pressure, I've drifted infield behind the ruck and find myself at first receiver. I take the pass from dummy half, Frano Botica. Initially, the task is to clear the line and, since there's no point trying to do that slowly, I set off at speed. I don't remember being more determined than usual, but I certainly don't hesitate. I accelerate and offer a little swerve as I reach the Leeds defence.

I remember drifting across field as I'd done on many occasions in the past, searching for a chink of daylight in the Leeds line. Suddenly I sight a gap and glide through it. A defender has a lunge at my ankles and misses. Neil Harmon, the Leeds prop forward, is closest to me, and he gets the 'big don't argue' in the chest. I'm really motoring by then. All he can manage is a gentle touch with his left hand. I'm through the line. Now there's space ahead and a swerve takes me through into clear air. I must be flying because the Leeds defence just seems to disappear behind me.

The run is still on a slight diagonal. I swerve a couple of times and there's no one near me. It seems that Sean Edwards didn't make the pace this time! There has to be a first for everything!

Alan Tait, however, is ahead, and he's known for his pace. It feels almost as if there's time to negotiate. I'm well right by now, heading towards the touchline. I swerve inside, but Alan is staying determinedly infield, offering me the touchline and a straight race to the line. He offers the challenge, perhaps because he's aware that there's a whole field of space if I can cut across to my left. I was already known as a winger who could go round almost anyone if there was open space. But this time I take on the challenge and accelerate decisively to the right, now going for it full throttle on Alan's left, on the narrow side. It's a classic duel.

What seems like an instant to an observer seems to me to last an age. I touch down near the corner. Alan Tait doesn't lay a finger on me. I've run 95 metres. Not one of my teammates has got anywhere near backing up. I get straight to my feet. I am already up by the time Alan Tait reaches me. Alan, the true professional, gives me a congratulatory pat on the back.

I sank to my knees, head in hands. The significance of the try had just started to sink in. I was flat on my back before any of my teammates arrived. I could hardly believe what had just happened. Listening to the match commentary now reminds me, however, that I should never take anything for granted. Ray French also noted that the gossip a month before the final was that I was out of form! He also immediately recognised the achievement as one of the finest the great stadium had ever seen. Later, he upgraded his assessment!

A newspaper report a couple of days after the final

suggested that I had to keep going because I had no one to pass to. Makes it all sound so easy! At the time I'm sure I knew I was clear of everyone except the fullback. But, in the game, what's behind stays there. It's what's in front that matters.

Given the angle of the run and the fact that I jinked and swerved, I covered more than 95 metres on that run. I was also watching the opposition and, don't forget, I was carrying the ball as well – at least I hope I was! And that sprint lasted, at the outside, twelve seconds: twelve seconds of history. I'd gone the length of the field. I'd done it at Wembley in a Cup final and I'd done it to make the first score of the game to relieve the pressure on my team.

Then, when all of that has sunk in, you start to think of all the other players who've done something similar. Stuart Wright for Widnes, Tom van Vollenhoven for St Helens, and Billy Boston for Wigan. But Billy Boston never did a length-of-the-field try in a final. The famous 1961 try by Tom van Vollenhoven was an inter-play between himself and his centre, Ken Large. And Stuart Wright's 1984 try effectively stemmed from an interception. Then it sinks in. You've lived a dream.

When I look back, I see what an individual effort it was. I did all the work. I kept going. And the line came to me.

But when I reflect on the experience, I begin to appreciate the luck, as well as the skill in a score like that. It makes you think of all the great tries that got away, the spectacular scores that didn't happen. My 1994

Wembley try made history and is now perhaps a permanent part of the game's folklore. It's part of the new Wembley as well, because there's a bar named after it! It's called simply 'The 1994 bar'. And the plaque reads 'named after the greatest try ever scored at Wembley'.

But if Neil Harmon had been one inch further to the left, if Alan hadn't showed me so much of the outside, if I hadn't come infield right at the start, then perhaps it would never have happened. You can have all the skills, the speed, strength, tactics, teamwork and stealth, but it still has to be your day. And April 30 1994 was my day.

2 & 3 – Ellery Hanley

Tries that go the length of the field are always spectacular, but only some of them are great tries. We have all seen games where one side is completely outclassed, the David and Goliath encounters that go predictably to form. When the victors' points tally hits fifty, or perhaps sixty or more, just about the only people left interested, certainly the only ones still cheering, are supporters intent on wallowing in their team's superiority. When your team has all the speed and strength, the tactics and the teamwork, it's easy to dominate another that has little of anything. Perhaps that's why such a large proportion of my greatest tries are scored on big occasions, when teams are finely matched and contests are keener. The game's history tells us that those big days can often be great levellers, ensuring that most such games have the competition, the nervous edge that can generate great play. So, for my next nominee for

50 Of The Best, I want to visit the Wembley Stadium of old and another Cup Final day.

The match in question was an important one for me. The try I'm about to describe helped to develop my own play. From it I learned a couple of things that proved useful throughout my career. The first was that you only have to run as fast as the players chasing you if you want to score a try. The second, and Ellery Hanley was a master of this, was, 'Keep going and eventually the try line will come to you'.

People are often surprised when I use that phrase. It takes them aback. A mild confusion often sets in prompting a quiet hesitation before they ask their question to clarify the phrase. "Surely when you are playing, you go to the line. The line doesn't come to you..." What I then usually do is repeat what I just said. "If you keep going, the line comes to you." From short yardage it's fine to go for the line. But from long range I've seen many players go for it with clenched teeth only to crash and burn as they tighten up. You only had to watch Usain Bolt smash the 100 metres world record recently with a run of 9.58 seconds to see how the line comes to you.

The year was 1988 and I was still learning about the game. I'd made my move into rugby league the year before, so I was still a rookie. And it's also worth remembering that rugby league changes very quickly. You can be an old hand and a successful one too, and a small rule change or new emphasis in the game can force you to re-think the way you play. The recent decision to abolish relegation and promotion in Super League, for instance, means that for three seasons, coaches, directors and players must re-think their approach to the game. The pitfall to be avoided for Super League clubs now is not a string of defeats leading to relegation in the short-term, but an inability to use this opportunity to build for the future.

Just how much the game has changed is illustrated by the context of my featured try. When Wigan played Halifax in 1988, it was only the second million-pound final. It was an era when many players, especially in the smaller clubs, were still semi-professional. Even some of the wealthiest clubs were not one hundred per cent professional. Times have changed, for certain, but when we look back at those twenty years, the quality of Ellery Hanley's try in that final is undiminished.

Like me, Ellery Hanley has been honoured for his contribution to the game. He was awarded his MBE in 1990. While I have the honour of scoring more tries than any other English player, Ellery Hanley has the undeniable kudos of being voted the greatest player of all time. He gave his nineteen years of service to Bradford Northern, Wigan, Balmain, Western Suburbs and Leeds and then coached Great Britain, St Helens and Doncaster.

Ellery Hanley has been around, and wherever he's gone he's brought his own special brand of commitment, strength, determination and character. What he did not bring a lot of, however, was speed. Don't get me wrong, I'm not saying that Ellery Hanley was a stroller. What I am saying, however, will be illustrated in my description of a try that has all the speed, strength and teamwork you could want. But it's finished with pure stealth, and Ellery Hanley's technique taught me the golden rule: "If you keep going, the line comes to you."

It's the 1988 Challenge Cup Final between Wigan and Halifax. Halifax are ready to re-start the game after the interval. They have made a substitution. Dick Fairbank has just come on and, as he takes his place in the chasing line, his team kicks off.

The ball goes to the left, deep to the Wigan right. Ten metres from the line Andy Gregory takes the ball on his shins and then picks up. He plays a short pass left to Joe Lydon who is already on the move infield, anticipating the pass.

After gaining ten metres, Joe dummies and takes a little step off his left foot before accelerating. His marker buys enough of the dummy to reduce his contact with the Wigan fullback to an ineffective left-hand slap as he passes by at speed.

Lydon heads for the gap behind the beaten defender. He rounds a second tackler with sheer speed and now has found acres of space.

But, though he straightens a bit, his opportunity takes him consistently further to the left. As he crosses halfway, his diagonal has taken him to ten metres from the left touchline. By now, Wigan have three players – not one or two, but three! – backing up to Lydon's right. The cover defence is also coming back. When Ellery

Hanley takes Lydon's perfect infield pass, he is on the Halifax 20-metre line. A combination of speed and teamwork have taken Wigan 60 metres upfield. From here, however, Ellery Hanley marries strength with pure stealth to score the try.

He's 20 metres from the line and has the Halifax winger, Graham Eadie, in close attendance. And Eadie seems to have the jump on him. Instinctively, Ellery changes body shape. If he goes straight for the line, Eadie will quickly overhaul him and get in the tackle. So he does something absolutely brilliant.

He sets off inside!

He's actually running sideways. The route he takes is much longer than going straight. He ends up running about 30 metres when the direct route was at least ten metres less. His progress towards the line is so delayed that he even collides with one of his backing-up teammates, Shaun Edwards, before he reaches the posts. It's almost as if his support is ahead of him by the time he scores under the sticks!

But the important point remains that Ellery Hanley was completely focused and in control. By running at an angle he could turn almost to face Graham Eadie, his pursuer. He could keep his body angled away from the tackler and use his strength to hand off, to fend off his tackler. In that way he knew he could keep going and, if you keep going, eventually the line comes to you. It's like slow motion played at speed. And the try sealed the game for Wigan. I learned a lot that day. Keep going and the line comes to you.

When talking about a figure as familiar as Ellery Hanley, it's easy to forget that he signed for Bradford Northern as early as 1978 and left the club as long ago as 1985. It was in the 1985 season that he won *Man of Steel*. In those days, he was still described as a utility back, by the way, and had just completed a season when he'd scored 50 tries, the first player to do that since Wigan's Billy Boston.

Now, that left arm hand-off that he used to keep Graham Eadie at bay at Wembley was a skill he had right from the start. In rugby league we call it 'big don't argue', and when Ellery Hanley used it, it was always big and the arguments were short. Just take a look at his try for Bradford Northern against Featherstone Rovers.

Bradford pick up a loose ball five metres from their own line. The pass goes to Ellery Hanley who takes the ball and heads off towards the right touchline. The Featherstone Rovers left centre lines up a tackle near the 20-metre line. Ellery gives him the left hand 'big don't argue' and even gets a little push off his tackler, adding to his momentum.

Tackler number two comes across. Ellery is now hard up against the right touchline. Hand-off number two despatches him. Ellery makes a complex skill look easy, and there isn't even a suggestion that he might lose his balance.

Next across, on halfway, is the fullback. Surely all he has

to do is hit hard with a crash tackle and Ellery will be in touch. But there's the 'big don't argue' again. By the time he's reached ten metres into opposition territory he's on his own. He's in the clear and the line comes to him. Magic skill!

It sounds so easy, doesn't it? The tacklers confront you and you apply the hand-off to send them flying. But all of this is done running at full speed along a touchline where a deviation from the straight and narrow by the width of a boot will take you into touch.

What's more, the tackler is also running flat out. He's a big guy, weighs a hundred kilos and is as hard as nails. To do what Ellery Hanley does needs amazing strength married to perfect balance. In his case, his strength in particular often made up for the yard of pace he lacked. And, for most rugby league players, strength is something you develop through hard work and dedication. Not everyone, including Ellery Hanley, is lucky enough to be born with it.

My personal relationship with Ellery Hanley over the years has been both close and important. It was on the 1988 Great Britain tour of Australia that we first got to know one another well. After Shaun Edwards left because of injury, Ellery and I became roommates and mates, as well. He took me under his wing, but I wouldn't embarrass him by calling him a father figure! He became more of another older brother, a mentor from whom I learned a lot. It was Ellery who gave me the sound advice that, as a player, you have to be thoroughly ruthless. But he also showed me how to switch it on and off like a light and how to relax before games so you wouldn't burn too much energy.

But he also reinforced some basic life lessons, such as the fact that rugby league clubs are your employers and don't necessarily have your best interests at heart. They look after themselves, so you need to look after yourself. In my first season in the game, he also reminded me that playing days come to an end and that I should plan for my future. Make hay while the sun shines, he said, and invest your money to prepare for retirement.

I'd only been in the game for a season, and this sound advice from Ellery was just what I needed. And I'm now passing on what Ellery taught me, plus some more, to the young players I represent and mentor: players such as Richie Myler, Kyle Eastmond, Will Sharpe, Tony Clubb and Mike Worrincy. Of course, I was already aware of most of these ideas, but Ellery reinforced them, helped me think things through and prioritise.

We saw quite a lot of one another when we got back to England after the 88 tour. Fans of *House Music* will remember that it was the *Second Summer of Love*, the birth of *House Music*, which has played a big part in my life ever since. And it's the source of my interest in being a DJ.

Ellery was the first person to take me to the iconic Manchester House club, *The Hacienda*. He opened my eyes up to a whole new world of jumping to the front of queues, getting into clubs free and rubbing shoulders and socialising with celebrities like Boy George, Mark

Moore from *S'Express*, Mike Pickering from *M People*, and Mick Hucknall from *Simply Red*, who is still a friend to this day. We were out together so much that people still come up to me today and ask, "Where's Ell?"

Ell taught me that you can have fun on a night out, stay sober and still get up in the morning and train hard. It's something I carried on doing for most of my career. Ironically, when I moved to Wigan, Ellery had just moved to Leeds and we grew apart as I became my own man. I was the old hand by then and it was me who introduced younger players at Wigan like Wes Cotton and Sean Long to the delights of *The Hacienda*! Thanks for the memories, Ell!

4 – Lesley Vainikolo

There have been some players in the game who seemed to epitomise strength. As we shall see later, forwards like George Mann used their immense strength to contribute much more than mere physical presence in a game. Strength is an indispensable quality in a team. Every player has to have his share, but the game always demands one or two players in every team whose strength is their main asset. They have to be mobile as well, of course, because it's when strength is combined with speed and mobility that defences are drawn in to leave gaps elsewhere. When we see such players handing it out occasionally, we must never forget that they usually become targets themselves. George Mann's career, for example, was ended by a high tackle that inflicted serious facial injury.

There's another position on a rugby field where perhaps paradoxically strength often rules, and that's on the wing. Over the decades, there have been some amazingly successful wingers whose speed combined with immense strength to overcome opponents. Jonah Lomu and Va'aiga Tuigamala come to mind. Let's not forget that the great Billy Boston himself, in his later years I must add, was pretty much in this mould and his size and strength were things that Wigan sometimes used tactically. In the early 1960s, when Wigan played Wakefield Trinity, the team of the moment in those days, more often than not Billy Boston's name was a team change from the line-up printed in the programme. He would move from number two to number three, to stand opposite Wakefield number four, the great Neil Fox. The only item of debate was then how long it would take for the first crash tackle to come in!

In recent years, the player most obviously cast in the 'power winger' mould has been Lesley Vainikolo. What's more, his career illustrates an aspect of the game that has really developed since my career ended. Lesley Vainikolo's rugby career has been international and all-embracing, crossing both codes and nationalities.

He was born in Tonga in May 1979, but grew up in Auckland, New Zealand. He played union as a youngster, but was already playing league as a teenager. His hero was the great Australian centre, Mal Meninga. Well, we are talking about strength and power...

His professional career began in 1998 with Meninga's Canberra Raiders' side in Australia. It was there that he got the nickname 'Volcano' which stuck. By the time he left rugby league in 2007 there was little else he could achieve. In five years with Bradford Bulls he had amassed a hatful of honours and had scored 149 tries plus one goal in 152 games. He was perhaps the last of the great try scorers.

Like all big strong powerful players, he has had his brush with injury. Impacts are felt on both sides of the contact, and complications can build up. But when Lesley Vainikolo was on song, the spectacle was awesome. Take this try against Leeds as an example. I won't name the Leeds defenders. They did nothing wrong. They were on a hiding to nothing on this occasion.

From a play-the-ball 12 metres inside the Bulls' half, left-side, Terry Newton picks up and goes down the blind side. He makes ten metres or so with a wonderful dash and then delivers a dream pass.

He squeezes between two defenders and then offloads left to his wing, Lesley Vainikolo. The pass goes around the defender on his left, not behind him. It's quite brilliant. Lesley Vainikolo takes the ball on halfway.

He's only trotting when he receives. He has had to wait for the pass, so he doesn't have much momentum when the Leeds fullback immediately comes across to cover. But, with a player like Vainikolo, it's usually useless to go in one at a time. The fullback gets in a tackle, but Vainikolo simply removes it. It's like he's wafting away an annoying fly. "Get off!" you can almost hear him say. But it's pure strength and power at work. By the time he's broken free he's facing his own line, running backwards! He pushes the defender off, like casting away an old sock!

A second Leeds player gets hands on him, but he suffers the same fate. Vainikolo simply removes him. Swats him away like a fly. By the way, these two players that have just been 'removed' are none less than Brent Webb, nickname Superman, and Jamie Peacock, six feet five inches, 104 kilos!

He can then turn and accelerate. There's no more cover ahead. There's only an uninterrupted run to the try-line. Quite simply awesome!

Though he's obviously worked at his strength and speed, Lesley Vainikolo was truly blessed. And don't forget that he's been timed over a 100-metre sprint at ten point something, so it's not as if his strength is his only asset.

There are aspects of Lesley Vainikolo's career that are going to form a theme throughout this book. Nowadays, players like him are rugby players, not specifically league or union players. They are just rugby players and able, via contract negotiation and residency qualification, to ply their trade across international borders.

Lesley Vainikolo played international rugby league for New Zealand. Though he qualifies by birth for Tonga, he's never represented Tonga in any competition. When he left Bradford Bulls he joined Gloucester rugby union on a significant contract. And by that time he'd already qualified via residence for England rugby union.

Since then, he's played five times for England, but surprisingly has yet to score a try. He is currently ruled out of the game because of long-term injury. Always remember impacts are felt on both sides of the collision.

5 – Gary Schofield

When I entered rugby league I was lucky enough to join a team with ambition, resources and a desire to win. And win we did, securing league leadership and championship wins in both of my first two seasons with Widnes, not to mention a World Club Challenge victory! To quote Robbie Paul, the motivation to keep winning comes when you remember how horrible it feels when you lose. I can't imagine how I might feel today if I'd gone 17 years in the game, playing most of them with top clubs, and never collected a single winner's medal in a major competition. But that's precisely what happened to Gary Schofield OBE.

Gary was something of a prodigy. He graduated to the senior game from amateur club Hunslet Parkside in south Leeds. It's an area that has produced a succession of talented rugby league players, including Jason Robinson and Kelvin Skerrett, besides himself.

In 1983 he captained the Great Britain youth team on their tour of Australia. When he came home he signed for Hull, the big spenders in those years, for £22,000, a vast sum at the time, especially for a player just entering the senior game. In his first season, he was the league's top try scorer with 38 touchdowns. But Hull finished second in the table, a point behind their city rivals, Hull Kingston Rovers. The same club also won the Premiership play-offs, and that year the Challenge Cup was contested by Widnes and Wigan.

In early 1984 he made his debut for the Great Britain senior side in a 10-0 victory over France. Gary himself described the match as the most boring he'd ever played in, and was convinced his international career would go nowhere. Now that is very similar to my own experience – a lacklustre game against the French and then being convinced that was the end of it. In my Great Britain debut, I scored a try and was still dropped for the return game against France in favour of David Plange. Mal Reilly was looking at his options, as he himself put it.

Gary went on to win 46 international caps, equalling the record of the previously most capped player, Jim Sullivan. The record still stands. And so in 1984 he was selected to tour Australia and New Zealand with the British Lions. He was still only 18 years old.

Two years earlier, the famous *Invincibles* had toured Britain and France and won every game, whitewashing Great Britain in three tests. They left a mark on the game, a mark that demanded greater commitment and professionalism, higher standards of fitness, more speed and strength, and – perhaps the most important of all – a thinking approach to tactics and strategy. Their superiority in all these aspects put them in a league of their own. Two years later, in 1984, the Great Britain tourists, under team coach Frank Myler and captain Brian Noble, set out to demonstrate that lessons had been learned and that standards had already improved. For a young player with only a season in the game, it was a big ask.

Well, of course we know it didn't happen. Not only were the tourists whitewashed again by the Kangaroos, they got the same treatment in New Zealand. During the tour and the test series, the Australian press carried stories about local players that were bigger than the ones covering the tourists and their international fixtures. The test matches were seen as a foregone conclusion. They weren't, of course, but they did largely conform to what, by then, had become an established pattern of a close game until the last quarter followed by an Australian flurry to record a comfortable win.

Australian journalists wrote some very unfair and unfavourable things about the British players, suggesting that for the most part they would not make the first team in most Sydney club sides. Two players from the squad, however, were exceptions to the rule, Ellery Hanley and Gary Schofield, both of whom scored tries in the tests, one in each of the first two for Gary and one for Ellery in the third. They were the tourists' only test match try scorers in Australia. Both of Gary Schofield's tries were exceptional.

At the time he must have come to the attention of Frank Stanton, the Australian coach. He was also coach at Balmain when Gary played with the club in 1986. It's interesting to read Gary's own description of Stanton's approach to the game. Gary Schofield admits that he tended to wander around the pitch a little, changing position during a game. Frank Stanton's approach was not to try to change his style, but to exploit it as a strength. Gary was therefore given a roaming role in the Balmain side. And it was a success. That season Gary achieved something no British-based player had done before when he finished top of Australia's try-scoring list.

For me, one of Gary's 1984 tries remains the best try he ever scored. It was an example of how speed and strength combine in a coordinated move that was pure teamwork. Gary's roving is illustrated perfectly. He figures no less than three times in that one move. He starts right-field on his own 20-metre line, receives again centre-field on halfway and finally touches down in the left corner. The whole sequence takes just 20 seconds.

Second row, Andy Goodway, plays the ball inside the Great Britain 20-metre line. Tony Myler is acting half-back. He picks up and suggests a drive to the right of the tackled player. He momentarily repels an Australian tackler with a hand-off and then turns almost to face his own line as a second tackler arrives. He gives a short pass to the right. The receiver immediately offloads to his right and Gary Schofield takes the ball for the first time in position at right centre. He is on his own 20-metre line.

Gary immediately moves the ball right again, because there's space for Des Drummond on the wing. Des makes 20 metres or so, drifting inside and jinking back to the right a little.

Schofield has followed. Initially he's on the outside of his winger, but as the defence musters and then threatens to smother the ball, Gary loops back inside. It's a crucial manoeuvre in the score, because it allows Des Drummond to use a short, safe pass, almost behind him, and also enabling Gary to take the ball at speed.

His pace takes him past one tackler and into space centre-field. But the defence is closing in again. To his right, he has support in the shape of – yes, you guessed – Des Drummond who has not stopped running since he offloaded. Obviously, if the Australian defence had taken him out of the game, the move would have gone nowhere.

Drummond advances and then uses support on his left from Goodway. Yes, it's the same player who played the ball back on the 20-metre line! The move has progressed 60 metres by now. And still there are defenders immediately ahead. Where on earth do they come from?

He in turn needs support and gets it in the form of Gary Schofield, who's now on the left wing. The pass is delivered almost immediately the ball is taken. It had to be to beat the tackle. Gary accepts it, goes full pelt for the line and just makes it at the corner, taking the flag with him.

The ball has gone through nine pairs of hands, three pairs of which belonged to Gary Schofield, and two each for Des Drummond and Andy Goodway. The try illustrates that the Great Britain players were both talented and capable. They could turn on play in bursts like this, but, as so often has been the case, they could not sustain the effort consistently and lost a lot of games in the last quarter.

There was much recrimination after the 1984 tour. Gary Schofield himself is on record saying what a shambles it had been. There were stories about squabbles within the camp that affected performances on the field. Even the Australian press, invited to some of the training sessions, commented on the lack of organisation. And, furthermore, Brian Noble's international career never recovered. It seemed the British game had learned little since the *Invincibles* tour. An image that perhaps summed up the mismatch was Gary Schofield's description of playing against the great Australian centre Mal Meninga. "He threw me around like a rag doll," said Gary.

Gary's time at Hull ended in 1987 after he'd been on strike in protest at his treatment when Gary Pearce arrived from Welsh rugby union. Hull fans have never forgiven him. He joined Leeds, his home-town club and stayed there until 1996, when he went to Huddersfield. In 1991, he had a strange year in that he was named *Man of Steel*, the league's most influential player, but at the same time new coach, Dougie Laughton, stripped him of the club's captaincy in favour of Ellery Hanley.

Late in his career he played for Doncaster and Bramley and also had a short spell in union with Aberavon. Perhaps Gary Schofield was unlucky. In his own estimation, he puts his failure to lift a trophy down to the phenomenal success and domination of Wigan at the height of his career.

The two tries of the 1984 tour remain exceptional. Gary Schofield's overall career was excellent, but unfortunately it wasn't brought to life by the success it deserved.

6 & 7 – Brian Carney

If there was any player whose career epitomises the changes seen in both codes of rugby over the last 15 years then that player would surely be Brian Carney. I've included two of Brian's tries in my *50 Of The Best*. Ironically, both tries came in the same game and both, if we're being critical, came from lucky escapes. When celebrating the skill and artistry of these scores, we must never forget that luck is always an element in our game. One of Brian Carney's tries was scored by virtue of excellent teamwork, while the other was sheer individual brilliance, match-winning stealth of the highest quality, but a stealth that could only be expressed on the back of complete professionalism, coupled with some luck!

The game in question is the 2003 Super League play-offs' decider. Leeds Rhinos met Wigan Warriors that night. It was second-in-the-table versus third for the honour of meeting league leaders Bradford Bulls in the Grand Final. It promised to be a close encounter, and so it proved.

Brian Carney's first half try illustrates how essential teamwork is in rugby league. Individual brilliance can only shine if the team provides a base for its expression. In this try Brian Carney's exceptional pace proves crucial. But it's only made effective through support play. The try also illustrates how fine the line is between success and failure. What could and perhaps should have been a Leeds score was transformed within seconds into a Wigan try.

The sequence begins five metres inside the Wigan half on the Leeds right. It's the fifth tackle and Andrew Dunemann kicks.

The kick is superb. It has height and is angled left. There's a gap in the Wigan defence and the kick is aimed there. Brian Carney has already dropped back to defend the touchline, but the ball is flighted to land significantly infield. The match commentators berate him for allowing the ball to bounce, but possibly this opinion does not do full justice to the quality of the kick.

Now we all know that coaching manuals say that you should follow up a kick with a level defensive line. It's part of the principle of teamwork. The player that fields the ball can beat people who arrive one at a time.

That's all very well if your prime aim is defence. What about if you have a real chance of being first to the ball? Well, of course, you'll go for it. And that's exactly what the Leeds centre, Keith Senior, does. In fact he gets to the ball first, just as it bounces. A pick-up is impossible so he lunges out with the boot. Even a tickle on the ball will almost certainly lead to a try for Leeds. The Wigan line is unpopulated.

But he misses and, trying to turn, slips. The ball bounces

into Brian Carney's hands and he's presented not with a defensive line, but with individuals in what is now a chase.

It's an understatement to say that Brian Carney was quick. In a chase, the chances were that he would win. And that's exactly what happens. He speeds past Kevin Sinfield and races along the Wigan right into the Leeds half.

Because play has followed a kick on a fifth tackle, there are teammates ahead of him who can support. But there's also plenty of cover arriving as well. Brian Carney has gravitated towards the winger's favourite place – the touchline – and he will be closed down before reaching the Leeds 20-metre line. Kris Radlinski is best placed among those backing up. When Brian Carney draws in the tacklers, he passes inside and Radlinski speeds on.

But by then the cover has appeared in numbers, and all coming from Radlinski's left. So his only route is to use the diagonal towards the right corner. He has the situation completely summed up however, because, in a completely unselfish move, he draws the tacklers further right and then throws an inside pass back along the touchline where Carney is waiting. Brian Carney seems to wait for the defence to pass like a train going over a level crossing before setting off. Then, from a near stationary start, he shoots through the gap to score. Professionalism and teamwork are the keys in that score, but it stemmed from a piece of luck when the kick was left to bounce.

Brian Carney and I seem to have quite a lot in common. Obviously we both played on the wing for Wigan. We both made our names in rugby league, but neither of us came from the game's heartland: I'm from London and Brian from Ireland. We both played rugby league because we wanted careers as professional sportsmen and we have both played a lot of rugby union. But Brian is ten years younger than me, and those ten years were crucial in terms of what opportunities were available to us.

Brian Carney was originally a Gaelic footballer. He played some amateur rugby league in Dublin, but his ambition was to join the professional game. He got his chance with Gateshead in 1999 and later played a season with Hull after the sides merged. At the end of that season he moved to Wigan. Again like me, he came to the attention of Wigan officials when he scored a try against the club.

He stayed with Wigan until 2005 and then went to Australia, originally bound for Gold Coast Titans, but eventually playing 26 games for Newcastle Knights. He retired in 2007, ostensibly to complete his legal studies, but immediately switched to rugby union, signing for Munster and being selected to represent Ireland on their tour of Argentina. After two successful years with Munster, he surprised everyone by returning to rugby league to play for Warrington. He was 33 by then, three years older than I was when I started to play rugby union for Bedford.

It makes me feel like an old man when I say things like

'in my era', but it has to be done! In my era, when a player switched from union to league, like Jonathan Davies, for instance, it was a one-way street. Rugby union would not re-admit a player who had turned professional. The change of rule came too late for me to have much impact on my return to rugby union. But for players of Brian Carney's era, just ten years beyond mine, you could start in union, switch to league, repeat the whole process and do it in reverse if you wished. How times have changed – and for the better. It's perhaps not long before we'll see league and union club sides under the same management umbrella at the same club, with squads assembled to maximise success across fixtures in both codes and some players in a league team one week and a union one the next. We'll see.

But I said there were two tries by Brian Carney from that game worthy of inclusion in my *50 Of The Best*. The second might get into anyone's collection. It's a try that epitomises how individual stealth and skill can win a game.

It was the second half of that same 2003 play-off decider. Leeds were ahead, but the game was still very much in the balance. A decisive score was probably going to win the game. And if you are looking for a decisive score, then Brian Carney's 90-metre effort certainly fits the bill.

But it still had its own element of luck. Kevin Sinfield kicks to threaten the Wigan line. It's another perfect kick, exactly what any coach might have wanted. It finds space. It too bounces, and more dangerously than the first half effort that Brian Carney turned into a counter-attack.

This time Radlinski has to collect the ball deep in the in-goal area. With the Leeds line approaching fast, he does something that probably wins the game for his team. It's as if he is scoring a try from close range. He takes a couple of paces and dives for the line – his own goal line! By diving, he makes sure that the tacklers can neither hold him up nor push him back. It also ensures that the ball will be grounded over the line and in the field of play. It's risky, even dangerous – and in some eyes possibly illegal! – but it proves a brilliant move. The ball is in play, less than a metre infield, but it secures possession by ensuring there will be no drop-out from under the posts.

There's one short drive to gain a few metres. When the ball is played, centre-field, just ten metres from the Wigan line, Brian Carney – now where on earth did he appear from to be dummy half centre-field? – picks up and runs. In fact, he runs straight at the tacklers. It's something like a forward's drive by a winger. All he's doing when he sets off is a simple limited job for his team. Gain some ground. Clear the line. But Brian Carney isn't a forward. He's both lighter and faster, so when he collides with the Leeds defenders, he literally bounces off.

Now a ball can bounce. It can bounce to your advantage, or it can destroy you. When a rugby ball bounces, don't bet on the result. Just watch and react. When Brian Carney runs at the Leeds defence at full pelt, they are ill-prepared. Perhaps they expect a conventional forward drive. Brian Carney's speed is therefore an unexpected complication. He can be knocked to the side, and he is, but he gets his bit of luck and is not going to fall over. So when he bounces off the tacklers, he finds himself in the clear.

He pulls away with spectacular explosive pace. Over the next few seconds it seems that the arms of every Leeds player stretch out towards him. Carney evades them all. He leaves everyone for dead and, amazingly, seems to be still accelerating when he touches down under the posts.

That try eventually won the game for Wigan. But it also shows several important things about rugby league. First, the boundary between success and failure is wafer-thin. A kick that bounced in the first half could have been Brian Carney's own and his team's downfall. It didn't happen. He countered and became a hero. A kick that bounced in the second half also could have gone either way. It eventually went Brian Carney's way and, as a result, he scored one of the few tries that could challenge my own 1994 Wembley try as the greatest ever!

8 – Clive Sullivan

At the start of my *50 Of The Best*, I said that the featured tries would all come from the last thirty years. I also stated there would be precisely three exceptions because I've included three tries from decades before 1980. My reasons are merely because each one, in its own way, has a historic element to it.

You're probably now assuming that because I'm a

winger and third on the all-time try-scorer list that I'll feature a score by Brian Bevan and another by Billy Boston. Well, you would be wrong, because I've chosen to include neither of them for two reasons. Firstly, I don't want to suggest comparison between them and myself. We operated in different eras of the game and thus our individual efforts should stand alone. Secondly, in my *50 Of The Best* I want to feature scores that have a story associated with them, either because of the stage on which they were set or because of the players involved. Personally, I know nothing of the Bevan and Boston eras. Neither can I remember anything about the three tries I've chosen from before 1980, but their stories are both significant and interesting. Many people with an interest in rugby league will at least be familiar with them, but I include them in my collection because their stories are good enough to be retold.

The year was 1972 and the venue was France. Now if there were any justice in the world, that information alone ought to generate vivid pictures in your mind. If I had just said that the year was 1966 and the venue Wembley, then even people of my age would know we were talking football, England and World Cup. So let's try again. It's 1972 and we're in France.

Well, it's the last time that Great Britain won the World Cup. In that tournament, Great Britain's players were undefeated in four matches. In the group stages they beat Australia 27-21, France 13-4 and New Zealand 53-19, the tournament's biggest win. The play-off against Australia finished a ten all draw – even after 20 minutes of extra time – and Great Britain won the trophy by virtue of having won all their group matches. The captain who lifted the World Cup, and a scorer of a spectacular try that day, was Clive Sullivan MBE.

Clive was one of the greatest players the game has ever seen. His origins were quite similar to Billy Boston's in that both were black, were born in Cardiff and were brought up on rugby union.

Clive was born in 1943. His ambition was to be a professional rugby player. At 17, he had a trial with Bradford Northern and was rejected, but then he signed for Hull. How could Bradford have not noticed his talent? Well, it has to be said that there might have been question marks over Clive's fitness. That was probably their reason for saying no. It proved to be a gigantic mistake. From the moment he took the field, Hull fans started telling the rugby league world that they'd signed someone quite special.

But his childhood had been rather strange for an athlete. His early years were blighted by problems with his body, especially his joints and his legs. He had severe problems with his knees, problems that needed surgery. He also had operations on his feet and shoulders. And here was a lad who wanted to be a professional sportsman!

It has to be said that Clive's career was dogged by injury. In the 1962 season he had three operations on his knees. At one stage, he even suffered a near-fatal car crash, but was back on the field in the first team three months later.

Clive played for Hull for 13 years and then did

something that surprised everyone. He moved east to join Hull Kingston Rovers. Now you might have thought that deserting to join the local arch-rivals would have angered at least half the city. It did at first. But Clive and his dedication to serve his club rose above it all and soon he was again admired and respected by all. He was a diplomat, a true gentleman, a fine leader and one absolutely stupendous winger. He scored 406 tries in 639 appearances during his career. And who knows? With fewer injuries he might have achieved the 500. He stayed in the game for many years, but died of cancer in 1985 at the age of 42. In Hull, part of the approach to the Humber Bridge is called Clive Sullivan Way. There's even a play about his life and career, written by Dave Windass and performed by the legendary Hull Truck Theatre. Now that's celebrity!

But the thing that Clive Sullivan ought to be remembered for is holding up that World Cup trophy in 1972. I hope that the inclusion of his try in my *50 Of The Best* will go some way towards achieving that greater recognition for the first black Briton to captain a national side – in any sport!

The rugby league World Cup has had a chequered history, however. It has been contested since 1954, when it was held in France. Great Britain won that first tournament. They won again in 1960 in England. The last time they won was 1972, Clive Sullivan's year. Australia won it every other time it was contested until 2008, of course. The England team entered that last competition with high hopes, but they came to nothing. The world of rugby league, however, was lit up – even set on fire! – when New Zealand beat Australia in the final.

There's a feeling in the game that the World Cup is a real competition again, with teams matched more evenly than for some time. In addition, with the expansion in the game in recent years, the splitting of Great Britain into home nations and the emergence of teams from several other countries, the tournament is now more varied, with many more possibilities of providing entertaining spectacle as well as serious competition.

It's a real achievement for the sport's governing bodies to have already agreed a format and venue for the next contest. It will be held in England in 2013, five years on from the last tournament to avoid clashing with the London Olympics. If there ever was a challenge capable of motivating rugby league players, coaches, clubs and administrators to improve their standards and performance, then surely this is it. In my opinion, all involved should focus on a home nation victory in 2013. It would be wonderful for the game.

So why didn't that 1972 triumph lift the game? Well it did, but forty years ago the British game was completely concentrated in its traditional heartlands in the north of England. Though there was television coverage, it was watched mainly by the sport's existing fan base. The wider public remained ignorant of rugby league. Even fifteen years later, when I got my phone call from Eddie MacDonald, Doug Laughton's assistant at Widnes, suggesting I consider playing the game, I really knew nothing about it. I had to watch games on television to get an idea.

Also the 1972 tournament was in France where rugby league is as regional as it is in Britain. When it became clear that France were not going to reach the final, local interest evaporated. But rest assured none of this would have reduced in any way the level of commitment or the desire to win amongst players in the games themselves.

I think 2013 will be different. All of us, fans and casual observers, professional and amateur alike, have to ensure that the next World Cup is a success for the British game.

So, having already made an exception to include Clive Sullivan's try against Australia in 1972, I now make a second one, because it was an interception try, well, an interception of sorts. But, didn't he motor!

It's the first half. There are two Sullivans on the field, by the way. Clive is on the Great Britain wing. Gary Sullivan is the loose forward for the Kangaroos. Two Great Britain forwards, David Jeans and Brian Lockwood, have just completed a smother tackle after an Australian forward drive by legendary second row forward Arthur Beetson. Play is 20 metres from the Great Britain line. A play-the-ball follows. This is the fourth tackle, so there's plenty of attacking scope left in this phase. The defence needs to stay solid.

The Aussies elect to move the ball wide rather than drive on. They play two passes left. Australian prop Bob O'Reilly tries to offload as he is upended in a fierce tackle. There's a support player coming up on the rush. It's none other than Graham Langlands, another Aussie legend, captain that day and, crucially, fullback. He can't gather and the ball dribbles forward. It's the power of the tackle that dislodges the ball.

The ball squirts towards Clive Sullivan, who picks it up and sets off straight. He's ten metres from his own line and the Aussie right winger, John Grant, is ahead. Sullivan goes right, heading for the winger's favourite spot, the touchline. It's a fast decisive sidestep. Clive Sullivan was a tricky winger as well as a fast one.

Commentary on the game was delivered by Eddie Waring, who at one time was known as the voice of rugby league. Now Eddie wasn't always the fans' favourite. He tended to be somewhat behind the play and clichéd. He did a lot to promote the game, however, and he did know something about it. Eddie's commentary is interesting at this point.

Clive Sullivan has just picked the ball up and set off. But Eddie, just like Clive Sullivan, knows that Graham Langlands has just been caught out of position at the breakdown. Immediately, Eddie suggests that Clive could go the length of the field. And that's exactly what he does, first heading for the touchline and then staying close to it.

He first sets off straight and then steps off his left foot to wrong-foot Grant, round him and get to the touchline side. He almost seems reluctant to step away from the line, even when he reaches the try-line.

After bending to pick up the ball and a standing start, Clive Sullivan places the ball over the Australian line just 13 seconds later, after a curving run. The Australian cover actually gives up running.

It was a classic winger's try. No doubt Clive Sullivan scored many better tries in his career. But there was surely none greater in its significance and achievement. It's about time we all acknowledged what a great feat this victory was and, alongside it, grant Clive Sullivan the same kind of national sporting recognition that we associate with figures like Bobby Moore or Martin Johnson.

But that's not the end of the story. Great Britain were actually trailing in that game by 10 points to 5 with only a few minutes left to play. Then they scored a late try that Terry Clawson converted to bring the scores level, force extra time, and eventually to take the trophy. The try was scored by the Great Britain hooker, a player from the unfashionable club of Dewsbury. His name was Mike Stevenson. Now I wonder whatever happened to him?

9 – James Roby

I want to use a try from recent years to illustrate some more characteristics of the modern game. Rugby league, as currently played in Super League, is a very different game from the one that Clive Sullivan played. It's probably even a different game from the one I played! Things have changed a lot in the last ten years.

The Wigan team I joined in 1992 was a fully professional team. It had just won the World Club Challenge, defeating Penrith. That side had two players from outside Britain and an Australian coach. The side that played

Leeds in the 1994 Challenge Cup Final in the game that remains so special for me had three overseas players, one of whom came on as a replacement. The Leeds side had just one overseas player at the start and a second who came on less than ten minutes from the end.

But the involvement of overseas players in rugby league is nothing new, however. It was the 1985 final that boasted ten overseas players on the pitch at the start of the game. But then that involved Hull, a team that, at the time, was something of a special case, because it relied heavily on imports by design. In the early 1960s, the great Wakefield Trinity teams were host to a procession of South Africans, Alan Skene and Gert Coetzer amongst them. And don't forget that Brian Bevan, he of the 738 tries from the 1940s to the 1960s, was originally Australian.

In the earlier days of the game, overseas players were few in number and those that made the switch tended to move and settle in their adopted country. Even in the mid-1960s, if a British player 'went to Australia', it usually meant emigrating and severing links with home and club. By the end of the decade things had already changed, but even when Malcolm Reilly from Castleford and Mike Stevenson from Dewsbury made the move, it was usually for good in relation to a career back home.

By the time I made my foray into the Australian game, it was becoming quite common for top players to turn out all year round by combining British and Australian contracts. The negotiation hinged around which hemisphere would get the major commitment. But then players were faced with the exacting challenge of being year-round sportsmen. Rugby league is a fast, tough game and makes tremendous demands on the body. A full twelve months a year in both training and competition is not something you recover from by doing it all over again! So even today, though they may be more flexible in the way they manage their commitments, players still have to decide how much, where and for how long to commit themselves.

In the 15 years or so since the mid-1990s, the people who now play Super League at the highest level have become truly international sportsmen. Even national identity is in some ways contractual.

My own position on this has always been clear. My parents were from Nigeria, but I was born and raised in London. I never thought of myself as anything other than British but of Nigerian extraction. I wore the Great Britain jersey 33 times and the England eight and was proud to do so on every occasion. But in modern sport it seems that nationality can be negotiable. Lesley Vainikolo is an example. He was born in Tonga and brought up on rugby union in New Zealand. After switching to league, he played for the New Zealand national side, but then wore the England shirt in rugby union. In no way do I make these remarks as criticisms. They are only observations on how the game and perhaps the world have changed.

In the Leeds and St Helens teams that contested the 2007 Grand Final, including interchange players and coaches, there were 11 overseas representatives. These were one

Samoan, three other Samoan-born New Zealand test players, two Australian-born New Zealand players, two New Zealanders, and three Australians. Of the home-raised players, one chose to represent Scotland. There could be no better illustration of changes in the game. Twenty years before that would have been a record. In 2007 it was not even worthy of comment. Our game has become globalised.

St Helens had finished league leaders in 2005, 2006 and 2007. They remained the most consistent and dominant team in the Super League. A member of their side, James Roby, was *Man of Steel* for the season. That Grand Final night, he scored an absolutely memorable try that summed up the changes the game had seen in a decade or more. And, for his labours, he finished up a loser.

But there was another aspect to James Roby's 2007 Grand final try that follows from my last point about the globalisation of the game. Having been recognised as the player who had had the greatest impact on Super League that season, James Roby started the 2007 Grand Final on the bench. In the past, this might have been described as being named a substitute, but in the modern game, this term simply no longer applies.

Nowadays, players who are on the team-sheet are almost certainly going to get on the field. And, as we all know, players can now interchange quite freely. Twenty years ago, when I was playing for Widnes, substitutions were made to replace injured players, and that's all. Nowadays the four replacements for each side are very much part of the tactics of the game. It's another example of how the game has changed to create hard-fought, balanced contests.

James Roby's try in the 2007 Grand Final is iconic in many ways. For me it epitomises so many of the differences between the modern Super League game and the older, more clearly regional, perhaps parochial game that I joined in 1987. So let's describe that try.

It's the first half and Leeds are leading 8-0. St Helens have already used some of their interchange players. James Roby is on the field.

Fa'asavalu is tackled. Note that there are four Leeds defenders in attendance. Smothering the ball is a must. Play is five metres inside the St Helens half, slightly right of centre. Roby is dummy half. He passes left to Sean Long, who makes a quick pass to his left to find Leon Pryce.

Sean Long follows his own pass, loops round Leon Pryce who was always going to be under pressure from an advancing defensive line. Pryce gratefully accepts Long's offer and gives a near-immediate reverse pass infield back to Long.

Sean Long then, in a stride, dummies left and steps right, straightens and accelerates. He makes a gap and then occupies it. He reaches the Leeds 40-metre line and cuts inside. The Leeds cover is about to smother him, but he has support in the shape of second row, Lee Gilmour, motoring up infield on his left.

Long passes inside and the receiver, Gilmour – a second row forward! – steps neatly inside a defender before the cover threatens to envelop him. The way out is a lobbed pass to the right on the 20-metre line over the heads of two defenders.

Roby takes the ball and makes a diagonal run to the right of the posts to score. He evades two tackles en route by sheer strength and momentum.

Now, in anyone's estimation this was a great try. It shows beautifully how teamwork, speed, strength and at least a little stealth can combine on the field to create both a spectacle for the fans and results for the players. In the context of the 2007 Grand Final, I use the word 'results' figuratively, of course.

And it has to be remembered that these four elements cannot combine without the fifth: tactics. The quality and vision of the training, coaching and management create a framework within which these talents can be realised.

So here was a try of the game's modern era. The handling was faultless. It went 60 metres forward, from right to left and back again. There was a loop pass, a reverse pass, two sidesteps (both right, but one by a second row forward), a dummy, searing pace, great strength and magnificent support play and – in the case of Sean Long at least – tremendous guile and stealth. There were just six passes in the entire move and, all the time, the Leeds cover made no obvious mistakes. I could argue that Roby should have been brought down short, but I'm already suggesting that he made the line on the merits of his strength, not the failure of a missed tackle.

There is another and, for this piece, my final comment on how the game has changed. When I joined Wigan in 1992, it was the only fully professional outfit in rugby league. As pros, we could devote our time to improving skills, building strength and speed, practising moves and everything else that makes the game. But back in the early 1990s, Wigan were the only side that could afford to do it with the whole squad.

In today's Super League, all players are professional. Standards now demand that players work at both speed and strength before anything else. A player that doesn't will not make the grade. Today, these qualities are on a different planet when compared to 20 to 30 years ago.

Professionalism also means that all players are better coached in all aspects of the game. Nowadays, tries are more often scored as a result of creative and inventive play than via mistakes by the opposition. No one can plan the run of the ball, of course, so there's always an element of chance to spice things. But in today's Super League, a player cannot afford even a single weakness in his game.

10 – Des Drummond

Anyone who has investigated references to my career on the internet will have come across the goalpost story. It's amazing how some quite obscure things become so easy to find and therefore so permanent, while some things of much bigger significance are lost completely. The story links me to a player I want to include in my *50 Of The Best*, a player called Des Drummond.

Now, Des Drummond and I have something of a history. I think it was in my first season in rugby league that our paths crossed significantly. He was by then approaching the twilight of his career. And it had been quite a career. We should remember that he only went to Warrington having already served ten seasons with Leigh where he played most of his rugby league. Even then, he had five years with Warrington, playing 182 times and scoring 69 tries. There was even a spell with Bramley after that.

He was an accomplished and distinguished player, appearing 24 times for England and Great Britain and scoring eight tries. As records go, that's right up there with the best. He was a tough, fast winger and, in the early days of my playing career, was the player I was most frequently compared to.

But he was quite a hard man, with a reputation for tough tackling. He was also something of a celebrity, appearing on BBC television's *Superstars* and amazing everyone with some of his performances. He finished runner-up in the 1983 competition.

As a winger, in his prime, he was fast, strong and inventive. Unlike many wingers who often like to hug the touchline, he was equally happy coming inside and stepping off either foot. He had a reputation for exciting play and doing the unexpected.

Now for Des Drummond's try in my *50 Of The Best*, I'm

not going to offer any detailed description. It's scored for Great Britain against New Zealand in 1984 and his finishing is clinical. There's a scrum ten metres inside the Great Britain half. The ball goes right. Des receives on the third pass. He's still inside his own half when he breaks through the gap. From the moment he sees clear space in front no one is going to catch him. He covers 55 metres to score. It sums up his no-nonsense direct style.

Remember also that Des played a significant role – two significant roles, in fact – in the Gary Schofield try I've already described. There was more to Des Drummond's game than the straightforward up and down the touchline.

But frankly, what I can remember in my early days as a rugby league player illustrates another side of the game. It's a side that is part of the game. Rugby is a contact sport and a player's physical presence on the field is part of the play. That's why rugby league players, if they are to make it in the game, must spend dedicated hours in the gym, building their strength and power.

Given this physical aspect of the game, it's inevitable that occasionally the physical contact will be too strong, that it will go beyond the mere push and shove of asserting your physical strength over the opposition. But rugby league has been very good over the years at identifying what is legal and what is not, and then putting in place systems that root out and punish foul play.

'Softening up' the opposition, however, remains part of the game. If you can get the opposition to think twice about making the run, going in for the tackle or taking the hit, you generate hesitation, split seconds that can only work to your own advantage. And I suppose it was a 'softening up' that I got when Widnes played Warrington. Every time I got near the ball it seemed that either Des Drummond or Les Boyd would launch themselves at me. I survived.

And that story on the internet? Well, the way it's written says that I and my Widnes teammates were celebrating a try. Des and his Warrington colleagues must have been a bit peeved. The story goes that Des decided to land one on me. The match commentator, Ray French, gave Des the benefit of the doubt by claiming that I had celebrated so energetically that I'd run into the post! Well, Des may have been something of a nemesis for me in rugby league, but when it comes to that particular incident, I don't remember a thing!

11 – Stuart Wright

When I entered the game, Des Drummond may have provided a role model for me to emulate as far as the wider rugby league community was concerned. For Widnes fans who came to watch their team at Naughton Park, however, there was only one pair of boots to be filled, if I were good enough, and those belonged to Stuart Wright. Though he operated along the right and I on the left, it was clear from the day I arrived at Widnes that all wing play would be judged against the standards already set by Stuart Wright.

Stuart's career was almost an exact opposite of my own,

and played out a decade earlier. Where I began with Widnes and then went on to a longer spell at Wigan, he started at Wigan and then won honours and glory throughout his 11 seasons at Widnes. When I arrived at the club, he'd just retired and was still very much a favourite. In 263 appearances he scored 151 tries and his pace was phenomenal. As evidence, take a look at the 85-metre interception try he scored against Hull at Wembley in 1982. In his length-of-the-field sprint, no one even gained ground on him. And if you don't rate interception tries, then take a look at his clinical close-range finish in the replay. Stuart Wright could score tries from anywhere, from distance or a 15-metre dash, cutting inside or hugging the touchline.

In many ways, Stuart Wright symbolises the game has changed in a generation. If my career straddled the part-time to full-time professional change in the game, then Stuart's career was conducted entirely in the older form of the game.

During his time at the club, Widnes was either at or near the top of the tree in rugby league. And just about throughout his time at Naughton Park, Stuart Wright was both first choice in his position and regularly a match-winner. But he remained semi-professional throughout. His trade was joinery. His part-time occupation was professional rugby league. When interviewed 20 years later by a local newspaper, he was still a joiner. When asked in the same interview if he thought he would have succeeded in the modern game, his answer was as definite as it was clear. "With my pace," he said, "I would have done fine."

The Stuart Wright try I've chosen for my *50 Of The Best* is the one that he himself recalls the most vividly. Like all players, he values the tries that won big prizes, were set on big stages and so provoke the strongest memories. In 1980s rugby league, the biggest stage was the Challenge Cup final at Wembley, and, of course, the first time you score there, and in doing so help your side lift the trophy, will always be the one that sticks in the memory. So, for Stuart Wright, former Widnes wing, I will again stretch my rule about including tries from 1980 and beyond because Stuart's first Wembley try came in 1979.

In 1982, the final between Widnes and Hull went to a replay. Stuart Wright scored at Wembley that year and also touched down in the replay at Elland Road, Leeds. David Topliss scored the winning try for Hull in the replay, a try whose sheer stealth and perfect execution would surely demand its inclusion in any selection of great tries. These two 1982 games were both spectacular and historic, but for Stuart Wright himself it was the 1979 game that was most memorable.

In 1979, David Topliss won the Lance Todd Trophy for his Wembley performance. And it was a performance for Wakefield Trinity, the losing team on the day. The score that put Widnes on top in that game came from Stuart Wright. It was in the first half and demonstrates another of the winger's skills that is rarely seen in the game these days.

The ball is in midfield, just inside the Wakefield Trinity half. Wakefield kick, thinking to chase. It's a poor kick, making only 20 metres or so and not finding space. On the day, every Wakefield Trinity fan rose to claim obstruction. There is a suspicion of a trip from a Widnes defender after the kick has gone.

Now, whether the referee didn't see it, saw nothing wrong, or whether he judged the kick already gathered, we don't know. This was an era before the video referee. What happens next, however, is that the Widnes fullback, David Eckersley, gathers and makes a short drive before turning to offload to Stuart Wright who's come in to support from the wing. He takes the ball just right of centre, about 15 metres inside his own half and initially sets off infield. Then he straightens and accelerates. By the time he reaches halfway, he's summed up the situation and seen the space beyond the defence. He is faced with a melee of players from both teams, because play has become compressed around halfway. There seems to be no direct path anywhere so the solution is to kick over the top into the vast space beyond and then run past the traffic.

If you're completely confident of your speed and there's space beyond the defence, it's a tactic that you can use. It's risky, because in a situation like Stuart Wright found himself, he has a full set of tackles under his team's belt. All he needs to do to receive the appreciation of his teammates is to field the ball, run straight, and get ahead of as many of his teammates as possible and then take the tackle. The play can then build from that new position. Giving the ball away with a kick on the first tackle doesn't usually make you popular!

But if you're sure of your pace and there are gaps beyond the defence, why not kick? And that's what Stuart Wright does. He kicks long towards the right corner. Then, without the handicap of carrying the ball, he exploits his amazing speed to the full and outpaces everyone to reach the target first.

Over 50 metres he's much quicker than anyone else on the field. He reaches the ball a couple of strides ahead of his pursuers. It's already bounced three times when he adds a gentle prod of his own with the boot to give it the extra couple of metres it needs to roll over the try-line. And then he touches down to score, outpacing no less than four cover defenders.

In today's game, I doubt you would see a winger – or any other player for that matter – try something that risky when their team had only just gained possession. Stuart Wright did it, and for him it came off. It was the first score and broke the Wakefield nerve. The game finished 12-3, but Stuart Wright's try was the killer punch.

The move was pure individual stealth, but made possible by pace. It had a lucky start when no penalty was given for obstruction on the Wakefield kicker. It had more luck in the way the ball bounced from Stuart Wright's kick. But then, as we see consistently throughout my *50 Of The Best*, luck is very much a part of rugby league and remains so to this day. The trick is to take advantage of it when it goes your way and to play on if it doesn't. But, as in many sports, if you have outstanding talent and make use of it, luck seems to go your way more often than not. Then it's not luck. It's talent.

12 - Playing football

Another try of my own illustrates the point I made earlier about interception tries and takes Stuart Wright's example of using a kick ahead to an almost ludicrous extreme. I scored a long-range interception try for Wigan against London Broncos at Brentford Football Ground in 1995.

Now, I suggested that even when they go the length of the field, interception tries are rarely memorable. That's because they arise from a breakdown in play and are converted largely through opportunism. In other words, luck plays a big part. Also, even a player without great pace can often go the length of the field after an interception because defenders are already committed to moving upfield and thus have to stop and turn to chase.

But despite this, I'm going to include one of my own interception tries in my *50 Of The Best*. In terms of quality, it's nothing compared to my 1994 Wembley try, but will illustrate an important point I want to make about the game and my approach to it. This try shows a combination of speed and stealth, but there were tactics involved as well, though the casual observer would never know. The try also came on the same evening that my tally passed 400. It was number 401. I scored four that night.

It was spectacular and lucky. It didn't go the length of the field, but managed three quarters. We are defending and our defence has been pulled to our right by some driving runs. The Broncos then set about moving the ball quickly to their right to find an overlap. There's more than a hint of space over on my wing. They have to move fast because our defence is quickly up to their line. The third pass after the play-the-ball is inaccurate. It's speculative at best, a lob in the end to avoid the approaching tackler. The receiver finds the ball way above his head and it goes to ground. If I want I can hang back, concentrate on defence, getting in the tackle when the player turns to gather. Instead I get a left boot to the ball by lunging a long leg forward. All speculative. Then something else comes into play.

It's an old-fashioned fly-hack from the 20-metre line. The Broncos have been on a concerted attack and have pushed up to our line. Thus my fly-kick pushes the ball into empty space – acres of it.

My pace takes me clear. The ball bobbles around so I kick it again. The chase takes me diagonally to my right as again the ball slithers across the turf rather than bounces. Of course, when you're not carrying the ball you can sprint at full pelt so, between contacts with the ball, I am pretty confident that there's no one on the field capable of catching me.

Now in a situation like that you need a lot of luck – a bounce of the ball to go your way. But for me it keeps going right and doesn't come up. It forces me more onto the diagonal, and slows me down relative to the cover defenders.

My third contact is with another left boot. It will just not come up to the hand and the ball goes even further to the right. That evening it seems the ball simply refuses to bounce.

By the time the fourth touch comes, the ball is far right, close to the touchline. I have to play it with the right foot this time. The contact is with the shin, actually, which on the night was my bit of luck, because the unintentional downward push causes a bounce. So, just as it reaches the line, it comes up. The defence has got back and I have a player in attendance when the ball comes to hand. By then, however, the try is not in doubt. All I have to do is take the ball and fall over the line. It was an opportunist's try, there's no doubt, the kind of try that gets the opposition fans shouting, "You lucky …..!" Now for the rest of the story.

If I claim the try illustrates stealth, then there must be some identifiable skills. In scoring that try, I made four contacts with the ball, all with the boot, three left and one right. This is not insignificant, but you can be sure I'm not claiming the ball control skills of a footballer. And tactics? How on earth can I claim there was any planning in a fly-hacked interception, even if I did go 80 metres on the diagonal from left to right?

Well, you'll have to take my word for it, but I regularly practised doing just that in training. I used to go out with the ball and get someone to chase me down the pitch while I fly-kicked the ball from one end to the other.

When you do it enough times, it becomes obvious that if the ball bounces up you take it. But if it doesn't, it's always better to kick again than try to pick it up. It's similar to the point I made about keeping going until the line comes to you. Picking up means stalling and that invites the tackle. If the ball is on the floor, all the chasers chase on equal terms and, if you reckon you're quicker, you'll arrive first. I was lucky that day, because the ball eventually bounced up and I could gather. But if you watch the try, you'll see that even if it hadn't gone to hand, it would have crossed the line and I would have been first there to touch down. Heads I won, tails I won, as long as I could control the kicks. And I could, because I used to practise exactly that. Yes, it was lucky, but a good part of that luck I made for myself through practice.

Since retiring I haven't seen anyone do that. I'd also bet that coaches these days don't encourage their wingers to practise fly-hacking. I reckon that in today's game, a player with an opportunity like that would opt to secure the percentage of possession after that first contact with the boot. Perhaps not. They'd probably take the defensive option, or just secure possession by falling on the ball.

13 & 14 – Henderson Gill

It's often said that rugby league lacks personalities. Equally this much-used term is used to identify people who, if we are merely accurate, have very little personality but a lot of presence. How many big-name footballers can you think of who regularly advertise something or other, clothing or fragrance, for example, or offer us car insurance or banking, model tight trousers or underwear, but who, when interviewed, string together the same set of small syllables? And yet we are told that these people are 'personalities'!

Perhaps the phrase ought to be written differently, to say that rugby league lacks celebrities, since people like the footballers I've just described are known just for their names, not their characters. They may be brilliant footballers, but their celebrity makes claims for them – often spuriously – in other areas.

Celebrities, of course, are created by financial or media interest and rugby league, still, is not a rich sport or very widely followed. Our game has few celebrities, but it's full of personalities. And one great personality who graced the game in the jerseys of Bradford Northern, Rochdale Hornets and, finally, Wigan, the club where he made his name, was a player called Henderson Gill.

I've included two tries by Henderson Gill. Both scores illustrate his combination of strength and speed, but both also arose out of teamwork. They were also both scored in a setting and context capable of making them iconic. One went down the left, the other on the right, possibly as a result of one being in the northern hemisphere while the other was down-under! But the tries are remembered not only for their skill, timing and spectacle, but also for what happened afterwards, which, on both occasions, was pure personality.

The Challenge Cup Final of 1985 has gone down in history as one of the greatest games of rugby league ever played. The match statistics alone tell some of the story. Wigan beat Hull 28-24. There were ten tries, five for each side. There were over 90,000 fans in the stadium that day and, when Wigan were apparently cruising towards victory, some of the Hull contingent may even have considered an early start home. I doubt it, though, because rugby league is a game that defies prediction, even, it seems, when things go to form.

Hull fought back and lost by just four points. Graham West, Wigan's New Zealand second row forward and captain, later admitted that they would not have held out if the game had been just five minutes longer. So, in the end, there was just one try between the sides and that day had been graced with a pretty special one. There was a real beauty by Brett Kenny, whose overall performance won him the Lance Todd Trophy, making him the first overseas player to be awarded the honour. In the second half, there was a frenzied dash to the line by a 'youngster' called Shaun Edwards. But there was one try that day that outshone them all.

In some ways the 1985 final was a milestone in rugby league. It was a game that now seems to lie on a cusp of change, where the old semi-professional game became something clearly of the past. At the same time, it anticipated a fully professional, fully international Super League future. There were ten overseas players on the field that afternoon. The star-studded Hull side had been assembled with financial injections over the previous few seasons and the club had become a real power in the game. There were New Zealand internationals, Gary Kemble, Fred Ah-Kuoi, Dane O'Hara and James Leuluai and, at scrum-half, Australian Peter Sterling.

Wigan, at the time, were newly emergent. A club with the highest quality of pedigree in the game, they had suffered some years of relative anonymity. But signings such as Australian *Invincibles* stand-off Brett Kenny, Peter Sterling's partner in the Aussie line-up and his teammate from Parramatta, pointed towards a successful future. The 1985 final began a decade when they were to dominate the game, a period when I myself, among others, came to Central Park as a big name signing. The Wigan side at Wembley in 1985, however, had not quite achieved such status.

Take our featured player, for example. Henderson Gill became one of the game's icons, installed in its folklore. He started with Bradford and was a mate of Ellery Hanley, no less. He always gave one hundred per cent in every game he played and he was never less than a completely willing servant to his team's cause.

But he is also one of the game's true personalities. His prodigious talent, his speed and strength, his skill, all these are indisputable. But like everyone else in life, he was not one hundred per cent successful, despite his talents and commitment. That's life, isn't it? But perhaps it's not celebrity.

What Henderson Gill had – and I am sure he still has it! – is a profound love of the game he played so well. And it's that love of the game that he expressed so wonderfully and memorably after completing the two scores I describe in my *50 Of The Best*.

So to the 1985 Wembley try for Wigan. It's the first half. There's a play-the-ball inside the Wigan 20-metre line. The ball goes left to first receiver Mike Ford, who had the unenviable task of playing opposite Peter Sterling that day. He feeds the ball further left to Wigan's brilliant Australian stand-off, Brett Kenny. He then opens up the Hull defence with a pass. It goes further left and finds centre, David Stephenson. It's a miss-pass that makes space for David Stephenson when he receives.

Stephenson was a hundred-per-cent dependable player. He knew centre play perfectly. As a winger myself, I know the importance of good centre play. The right player inside gives a winger both confidence and motivation. You know you're going to get good service.

David Stephenson takes his opportunity by sprinting into space before delivering a perfectly-timed pass to Henderson Gill on his outside. It puts the winger into space, but there are still 70 metres to go to the line and the try still has to be scored.

The Hull wing has come infield to tackle David Stephenson. Hull scrum-half, Peter Sterling, has looped around the tackle and is inches away from tapping Henderson Gill's ankles as he heads down the touchline. The match commentary notes here that, "...there is only the fullback to beat."

Gary Kemble, one of Hull's imports from New Zealand, was at fullback that day. Ray French just has time to ask the question, "Can he beat the fullback?" before the answer, "Yes he can!" describes what happened. Henderson Gill takes the ball and, with the complete single-mindedness of a try-scorer, uses both speed and strength mixed with dogged determination to round the fullback and score for Wigan.

It was a try that illustrated true teamwork, despite the fact that a casual observer might see it as a long-range, individual effort by the winger.

Brett Kenny was a play-making half-back. He certainly made that play, and made it out of nothing. His pass created the space that made the whole thing possible. David Stephenson's centre play was perfection for the role. A good centre is both powerful and skilful. But a good centre is also unselfish, bent on creating a better opportunity for the winger he supports. David Stephenson was able to draw in the cover and then put Henderson Gill in the clear with a perfectly-timed pass.

A winger's job is to exploit space along the flank and to score tries. You need speed and a good measure of highly specific skills. Gary Kemble was a world-class international fullback and Henderson Gill that day made a tough task look easy. No one was going to stop him and no one did. And he scored – and then he smiled. And what a smile!

This wasn't just a job done. This wasn't just a score to contribute to a professional demolition of an opponent. When Henderson Gill smiled at his teammates in Wembley Stadium, it was clearly a simple and sincere expression of achievement and pride, the knowledge that he'd done something special for a game that was his very life. Now that's personality.

And as a footnote to this great try, from the perspective of twenty-five years, let's bear in mind that Henderson Gill, on hanging up his boots, became a disc jockey and information technology teacher. His teammates that day, on their own retirements, did a complete range of things. One became a surveyor, another a building inspector, yet another a cab driver who had to care for an injured son. Two others, at opposite ends of the earth, found themselves in occupations as diverse as forestry and delivery-van driving. There were casualties as well. One player suffered a brain haemorrhage, and another a severed artery after breaking a collarbone in training.

The point is that rugby league is played by real people. What unites them is their passion for the game. Real people have real lives and real personalities, unlike celebrities who tend to be what the market for their commodity wants them to be. Incidentally, two other of Henderson Gill's 1985 Wigan teammates went on to do something that, at the time, had it been suggested even as a remote possibility, would have been laughed at as inconceivable. They went on to coach in rugby union, both eventually at international level and one of them, 'youngster' Shaun Edwards, to the very highest levels of the sport. How times have changed!

Henderson Gill's future as a disc jockey might have been predicted by those who saw his 1988 try for Great Britain against Australia in Sydney. Again it's a try remembered for its aftermath, but not, of course, primarily so. While his 1985 Wembley effort finished with a smile, his 1988 try in Sydney was followed by Henderson's now famous boogie.

We had kept our noses in front throughout the game. But in the second half, there was a period when things might have gone against us. All too often over the years, Great Britain sides have managed to stay in touch with the Aussies until the last quarter of the game. Had the Aussies pulled away and won that third test, history would simply have recorded that it had gone to form.

When Australia scored just to the left of the posts, they were again within one score. It was a close-range effort, a real grafter's try by prop forward, Sam Backo. It was a good season for him. He had registered on score sheets frequently that year. In three State of Origin games during May and June just before the July test match, he had scored three tries and been man of the match twice. So when his converted try brought the score back to 16-12, there was every possibility that the game might go the way of previous encounters. But it was Great Britain who scored next to stretch the lead to 20-12 and it was Henderson Gill's great try that put the confidence back in our side.

We were just 20 metres from our line. There was a play-the-ball on our right. Andy Gregory was acting half-back. He passed left to first receiver, Paul Loughlin. Now it was a pretty ropey pass. It was low and a bit short. Paul had to check back and also stoop to collect. If he'd spilled the ball, it would have been the pass that got the blame. And who knows? A scrum with an Australian feed just 15 metres out at that stage might have seen the sides at least level by the end of the next set of tackles. The margin between success and failure can be very slim.

But, having checked, Paul was now committed to going right because the Aussies' line was up. Who cares if the

Australian defence was just too keen and over-committed? Tony Currie lunged in and missed the tackle. Hooker Greg Conescu did the same. But Paul had accelerated and beaten them for pace. Ironically, it was Sam Backo who got closest to stopping his surge forward, but he didn't have the pace to prevent the break. "Loughlin just strode through the defence," said the match commentator.

He was now clear. Henderson Gill was in support on the right touchline. Gary Jack, the Kangaroos' fullback was ahead. The pass was well timed, but not perfect because Henderson still had work to do to round the fullback. "Can't this guy motor," the commentator said as he touched down in the corner with both Gary Jack and Andrew Ettinghausen nearby.

And then came the boogie. Henderson got straight to his feet and gave one of the greatest hip swivels in history to celebrate. I was first on the scene to congratulate him. Again the smiles illustrate the return of self-belief.

These two tries, one down the left, one down the right, one with a smile and one with a boogie, one for club and one for country, one at home and one away, were finished with speed, strength and teamwork, and, I'm sure you agree, with bags of personality.

15 – Mal Meninga

Teamwork is the very essence of rugby league. Every aspect of the game demands it. We always assume that professional players are fit and suited to the task. Players must have speed, strength and skill and, furthermore, must work at improving them throughout their playing careers. But teamwork is just as important. An individual's assets are essential, but not the whole story. Teamwork is vital.

At one level I'm stating the obvious. Watch any game for even less than a minute and it will be clear that every phase of possession and probably every tackle would be impossible without players working together as a team. It's one of the game's 'givens'.

But sometimes teamwork is much more than merely acting together. Sometimes it wins matches. We know immediately when we've seen it. Individually, skills and abilities are in evidence, but when teamwork wins matches, it goes beyond this. It offers a perfect example of a whole becoming more than the sum of its parts. Imagine two teams, both of which have strength and speed. There are individual skills and abilities in every position on the field. But sometimes there's also a blend, a perfect mix of talent and ability that enables a team to achieve something bigger than any individual could manage. I recall with some pain – literally – a perfect example of teamwork winning a game.

The 1990 Great Britain team had a victory under its belt when it took the field at Old Trafford on 10 November. We'd beaten Australia 19-12 in the First Test at Wembley. Once again, we were just a game away from an Ashes win in the best of three series. The last time that was achieved was 1970. Even when Great Britain won the World Cup in 1972, they only needed to beat

Australia once, because in that competition, the four participants, the Kangaroos, Kiwis, Great Britain and France, played each other just once before the final and that, of course, was drawn. All the players in Manchester that day were keenly aware of what they could achieve. And for the first time in many years, we felt that the glory was within our grasp.

And make no mistake about how keenly the Aussies compete on such occasions. All successful outfits make success a tradition, and it's a tradition that the players do their absolute utmost to preserve. Anything less than victory each time is a loss of face for those involved. In some ways it's harder for the Aussies. They are expected to win and, if they don't win, they have to live with the failure for the rest of their careers, perhaps for the rest of their lives. Ricky Stuart, who was to play both villain and hero that November afternoon, described his error that led to an interception try as like a 'death in the family'.

Things had gone quite well for us that day. In front of over 46,000 spectators we'd not only held our own against the tourists, we had outplayed them in several departments. Paul Loughlin had raced 50 metres to score after intercepting Ricky Stuart's speculative pass, an error in just his second international that might have threatened his career had he not made amends. With the scores at ten apiece, we had a share of the Ashes, and there was just a minute left in the game. We were that close to history. I was willing the guys on from the treatment table in the dressing room as a contact with the opposition had earlier helped to strain my medial ligament. Watching what unfolded on the dressing-room television screen while lying prostrate in pain will live with me forever.

That try which won the game for Australia was pure teamwork. It also embodied every other aspect of the game. Stuart's speed and step, Meninga's strength, the stealth of Lindner's reverse pass, the brilliant backing-up of Ettinghausen and Meninga all combined in one unstoppable mix. And tactics also played their part. How often do we say that a football game lasts for 80 minutes? Coaches are forever drilling the fact into players' heads. It takes less than 20 seconds to go the length of the field to win a game, as I know.

The scores are even at 10-10. Great Britain are in a good position. We have the Kangaroos on the deck just 17 metres from their line in front of the sticks. An Aussie commentator excitedly announces that there is almost no time left in the match. He thinks there's about a minute of injury time. The next five passes take less than half of that time.

The play goes left from the tackle and Ricky Stuart passes left again. Bob Lindner's stealth now makes something out of nothing. In barely a second, he's taken the ball and suggested a turn towards the left touchline before an immediate switch of direction with an unconventional reverse pass. The ball is obviously going left along with the player, but it doesn't. It goes back to the right and, as a result, there's the slightest of hesitations and, perhaps because of that, a missed tackle. Had that tackle stuck, we would have shared the series, at least.

Another quick pass right finds Ricky Stuart again and the commentator has time to announce that the game is in injury time. There are just 40 seconds to play.

Looking back almost 20 years later, it's hard to see events how they were, rather than what they became. It's possible that if Great Britain had snuffed out that move and shared the Ashes that the whole development of the game might have been different. But in the 1990 second test, when Stuart dummies right and then steps off his right foot to find a gap, he accelerates to top speed in an explosive couple of strides and then he's clear. Things are suddenly going well for him after his interception gaff.

I wonder what his reaction might have been if things had not gone his way that afternoon. When the Kangaroos lost the World Cup Final in 2008 to the Kiwis, Ricky Stuart was the Australian coach. He made history of his own at the time with his comments about the referee and others after that game. He later apologised for those insults and retracted his accusations, but he revealed himself as maybe not the best of losers.

But that November afternoon at Old Trafford in 1990 he's now in the clear and in control. He's just 15 metres from his own line when he receives the ball for the second time in the move and only a couple of metres further forward when he sells a dummy to Lee Jackson. A couple of seconds later and he is up to halfway. He said afterwards that he thought of kicking ahead for Ettinghausen to chase, but he simply speeds on. By now in the changing room I was almost sitting up screaming at the television, "No! Please, no!"

But there is cover closing in. Steve Hampson, the Great Britain fullback is ahead and has to be beaten and just behind there's Ellery Hanley, Andy Gregory and, closest, centre Carl Gibson in pursuit. On Stuart's left he has Ettinghausen coming up like a train and, behind, in amongst the pursuers, Mal Meninga.

Now Mal Meninga is one of those players who arouses strong feelings. If you're a teammate or a supporter, his status is God-like. For those on the opposition he's the satanic thorn in the side. 1990 was his first tour with the Kangaroos as captain. Had he not won that second test and handed Great Britain a share of the Ashes, who knows where his career might *not* have gone?

In the event, Big Mal captained Australia 23 times. He won every honour in the game. He was awarded the Order of Australia in 1994 and in 2008 he was named at centre, alongside Reg Gasnier, in Australia's greatest line-up, The Team Of The Century, chosen by a panel of experts to mark the game's centenary. His only foray into the British game was just one season with St Helens in 1980. Big Mal was an Aussie through and through, making his name in Queensland before winning premierships with Canberra Raiders. If you were in the opposition, Big Mal Meninga was a giant tough rock of a man who could completely dominate the centre-field, knock the stuffing out of you, run rings around and paths through any defence and, to add insult to severe injury, also kick goals. You knew when you'd played a game against Mal Meninga. He was nothing less than the epitome of speed and strength combined in a frame the size and shape of a tank.

In Old Trafford's second test, with just 25 seconds left to play, Mal Meninga is behind Stuart, hemmed in by Great Britain cover tacklers. Big Mal then does two things that win the match for Australia. The first is a nudge in the back of Carl Gibson, the Great Britain number four. A nudge from Mal is enough to take you out and Carl is propelled a couple of metres to his right. It's effectively an American Football block to protect Stuart. Then Mal cuts inside and accelerates. It's easy to forget how quick he was. In a couple of strides he's alongside Stuart, offering a safer option than the more distant Ettinghausen.

Stuart times the pass to perfection. Steve Hampson is committed to the tackle when the pass goes to Stuart's left. With Gibson still stumbling from the hit, Meninga heads for the line. The try still needed scoring. He has another assist when two Great Britain cover tacklers collide, but even their combined efforts would not have denied the score. It was a great try, a true team effort, a try that won the game and kept Australian hopes of winning the series alive.

The Kangaroos went on to win the third game and the series. Who knows how differently the game might have developed if those 40 seconds had seen three tackles in the Aussie half and thus a share of the series for Great Britain? I was hurting on the treatment table in my heart as well as in my leg. Knowing that the winning try had gone down the left, I was left musing on whether, if I had still been on the pitch, my speed might have enabled me to make the cover tackle on Stuart to secure the draw. It was all academic by then, of course. And the player whose impact had taken me out of the game? A certain Mal Meninga. He, not I, was now the hero.

16 – Doing the Offiah

You know when something in sport has become iconic. It doesn't have to be something spectacular, though it often is, but it does have to be something memorable. How often when we watch sport – whatever the game – do we say something like, "He's doing a..." or "That was just like...used to do."

Something done for the first time often gets labelled with its inventor's name. We all know what a Fosbury Flop is. A Biellmann Spin in figure-skating may be less familiar, but it's a technique named after Denise Biellmann, the first ice-skater to use it in competition. And, of course, just about every move in chess is named after someone. Doing a Maradona 'hand of God' in football may not be appreciated, but the phrase immediately conjures up a memory. Infamy like that, however, is not something that most of us seek.

So when I watched a recent Super League game between Hull and Leeds, I was immensely flattered to find that one of my own tries had achieved at least a little of that iconic status. When the Hull left wing found himself on a run against a retreating cover defender, he jinked inside and out and then threatened to do the same again. It prompted the Sky Sports commentary team to recall that a certain Martin Offiah once scored a try doing that. The difference between my effort and events of that evening was that the Hull winger fell over, tripped over his own feet, whereas in the original I scored. It was a try in a 1989 international against New Zealand, a try that mixed speed and stealth in equal measure.

Though we went on to win the series 2-1, it's a pity that Great Britain lost the First Test against New Zealand that year. It finished 24-16 in favour of New Zealand. But I remember that game in particular – as do others, it seems – for the long-distance try I scored.

We played the game at Old Trafford, Manchester in front of a crowd of over 18,000. It was an era when the Kiwis had become a real force. Many of their players already had several years of experience in top English sides, so they knew the settings and the opposition.

I can remember the try vividly. There was a play-the-ball about 17 metres from our own line in front of the posts. I was acting half-back for some reason. Don't ask! It's a position from which my teammates usually elbowed me away. But, you know, I always fancied my chances as a ball distributor. Well, in that game, I was acting half-back and I suppose, in some ways, I did distribute the ball. In fact, it went as far as the other end of the field, because I carried it there!

Initially I set off right on what turns out to be a dummy run. There are two tacklers nearby, Gary Freeman and Jim Goulding. The prop, Goulding, is rather tied up with my teammate. Scrum-half Freeman moves my way, but when I stop and go back to the left, he's stranded, blocked off by Goulding. Now I planned that… (There's a pause here to give time for a smile!)

But once I've gone back to the left, I have a gap. I have to go further left, and when I take a step off the left foot I'm already moving just too fast for the two tacklers from the defensive line that close in to plug the hole. I've straightened and gone for the gap, beating Kurt Sherlock. The line will come to you if you keep going! Kevin Iro has had time to come in from the right wing, however, and he lunges into the tackle. But he's off balance and I can hand him off with a little jab of the left hand. Believe me, handing off Kevin Iro is no mean feat! Now I have some open space ahead and can put my foot down. There's only 75 metres to go.

There's a cover defender ahead, the New Zealand number five, Gary Mercer. I do have some support to my left, but then there's acres of space to the right as well. I know that if I head to the right I can wrong-foot him. It doesn't work. I go right and so does he. I go back left and he covers. I go right again.

And there we are now within a few metres of each other. I try another shuffle and weave before cutting away decisively to my right. It's an exact example of what I learned from Ellery Hanley's try at Wembley – the shortest route is only sometimes the best. The one that gets you there beats the rest.

My jinks right and left had opened up acres to the right. I know I can speed up if I use that space. I know my pace will tell and that the line will come to me.

By the time it arrives, I'm well to the right of the posts, having run on a diagonal to my right over the last 25 metres. Mercer tries to follow. But by the time I get there I even have time to do a bit of a shuffle to celebrate before diving to ground the ball.

I'm now proud to have done something that sticks in people's memories. It was that repeated swerve that made the space and opened up the diagonal. It also bought me a metre or two of ground by confusing the defender, causing hesitation. It would be gratifying if the move became known as the Offiah Shuffle. The trick when doing it, of course, is not to fall over!

17 – Scott Grix

Modern rugby league is undoubtedly a very different game from what it was in the Bevan and Boston eras. Some people have criticised the game for being too willing to change. I don't agree with that. The only reason the game embraces change is to make the play more fluid, more open and generally quicker. In the days when a team had unlimited possession, a pack of forwards could 'shove it up their jersey' by means of a simple game of play-the-ball, pass to first receiver, drive and repeat. Generally, a team with a big enough and strong enough pack could usually wear down the opposition. Players didn't even have to be all that mobile, because most play was concentrated near the game line. If a break was made, of course, you still supported the player with the ball so then the speedier backs could be used. But generally there was little need to use the backs until the forwards had driven on to an attacking position. Also, there was little tactical kicking in those days, so the only time a winger had to defend deep was from a penalty kick to touch, Now devotees of the game from that era will deny all of this, I'm sure. But that's what it looks like from today.

But this all changed in 1966 when the four tackle rule was introduced. Instead of unlimited possession, teams got precisely four tackles. Suddenly teams had to find kicking skills. For a season or so, rugby league resembled a frantic version of kick and rush with most teams opting for the simple up-and-under on the last tackle. Soon new skills were learned.

Four tackles proved to be too few, however. Play became fragmented and there were too few opportunities to build positions. So the game changed again in 1972 when the tackle count was raised to six. It took six years for the game's administrators to decide that four was not enough and six would be better. It hasn't been changed since then. This clearly is not an over-eagerness to change. It was a managed, considered modification to the game designed to open it out and speed it up. Changing the rule again merely illustrates the game's ability to reflect on and evaluate change. It had worked, but hadn't worked well enough. Tactical kicking was, well before 1970, an essential part of rugby league.

But tactical kicking in the modern game is used for much more than gaining ground before possession changes over. Such skills have been a long time in the learning, but are now firmly part of the game. Though he was noted for many skills, Australian scrum-half Peter

Sterling developed a reputation for creating scoring chances with a short lofted kick to the wing. It's effectively a miss-pass with the boot. He probably wasn't the first person to do it, but during the 1980s when he played with Hull, his use of the tactic was much discussed – and copied!

A recent game between Wakefield Trinity Wildcats and Leeds Rhinos illustrates how much a part of the modern game it has become. Scott Grix scored the try, but it was a try that arose out of superb teamwork combining with Danny Brough's boot.

Wakefield are 22 metres from the Leeds line, just to the left of the posts. The play-the-ball follows the fifth tackle. In the old days the up-and-under would have been aimed at the crossbar. But not in the modern game.

Brad Drew is acting half-back and Danny Brough is first receiver to his right, virtually centre-field. Rather than pass, Brough lobs a kick to the right touchline. It's an excellent kick, weighted to land just inside the line.

Now in a competition for a high ball, the attacking player is running forward while the defender often has to wait. So in theory at least, the attacker ought to get up higher than the defender. That's exactly what happens in this case. Wakefield right winger Matthew Petersen takes the ball cleanly in the air.

But there is no opening on that side. The Leeds cover has funnelled across in an effort to smother play and force the changeover. So Petersen throws a pass back infield, to his left. It's a speculative pass that goes to ground. Luckily for Wakefield, it bounces once and bounces high. They are always going to retain possession – the pass was perfectly safe – but the kind bounce keeps the move alive as Dale Ferguson gathers. The next pass is again left, back to centre-field, back to Danny Brough. Just a moment, didn't he just kick the ball?

The Leeds defence is quickly onto him. He has to take an immediate step to the right to evade the onrushing tackler. He succeeds and thus makes some space.

Now you might expect – with one player just beaten and the Leeds cover favouring the Wakefield right – that he might drive on and look for a short pass to a support player. But no. There are two Leeds defenders straight ahead. So he kicks again, this time towards his left wing.

This time the kick is near perfect. It's flighted to land just infield, close to the left corner, but of course it never hits the ground. There's no Leeds cover wide on the Wakefield left, so Scott Grix can chase, take the ball and touch down almost unopposed. Match commentators ask the Leeds team, "Is there anyone at home?" because there are simply no Leeds defenders in sight.

The move went two thirds of the width of the field from left to right and then the full width of the field back to the left touchline. Seven Wakefield players touched the ball. There were three passes and two cross-field kicks, both executed with complete control, accuracy and a good deal of stealth on the part of Danny Brough. Those skills were largely unknown in the old game. Now that's change.

The try, of course, went to the video referee. In a matter of seconds he was able to check whether both chasers, Petersen on the right and Grix on the left, were onside when the ball was kicked. And they were. It was a great inventive try, created by pure stealth and skill.

The video referee is now an established, even essential part of the game. Though it does not settle every controversy, it settles the vast majority of disputed calls. Gone are the days, thank goodness, when games could be decided on a refereeing error. I am not criticising referees, by the way. But the video referee has illustrated time and again how difficult it is for one official with one perspective on play to make judgements.

The introduction of the video referee was just one more example of rugby league accepting the need for change and being willing to make that change. The case for using whatever technology is reliably available is now made. Not only rugby league uses such systems, of course. They are now regular features of many sports, but not football. What a pity they have not yet got the obvious message. If football had video referees, then just possibly the 'hand of God' might have been spotted. Let's continue to embrace change.

18 – Jamie Lyon

The next try in my *50 Of The Best* features Jamie Lyon. Now, St Helens have been blessed with a succession of great centres over the years – Meninga, Iro, Gleeson, Gary Connolly as well – and now they've got Gidley. And there were two seasons of Jamie Lyon. He set Super League alight with his eye for a gap and his ability to make the outside break. He wasn't a bad kicker either! In 63 appearances for Saints he scored 46 tries and 213 goals. He was really world-class, but when you look at his record overall, it might be that Saints actually got the best out of him. When he left, Saints were worried that they wouldn't be able to replace him, and then Gidley came along, so they did all right.

There's a couple of interesting aspects to Jamie Lyon's two seasons in Super League. The first is an observation about big-name Australian players who come to Europe. There have been quite a few over the years. A lot have lived up their big-name billing. Players such as Andrew Ettinghausen and Mal Meninga were great players anywhere. They are able to transfer their skills into the slightly different game we have over here. But both of these two great names gave only one season each to the British game and it's always easier to stand out when you're new. It's a different matter to repeat the success once your face is known. But there are some players who arrive with big reputations who don't live up to the hype. Some, like Ettinghausen and Meninga, come and go, whereas others, such as Phil Veivers, stay longer.

In Jamie Lyon's case his contract was for two years and that's what he did. He was one of those Aussies who comes into Super League and fits in immediately – a hit from day one. Voted *Man of Steel*, he found a place in the Super League Dream Team in both seasons.

But then I suppose we shouldn't underestimate what a challenge that move can be. There's always a lot of pressure on a player who comes with a reputation. It's the same for a British player who goes to Australia. After all, rugby league is a team game. It's not about one man. You have to fit into a team and its structure. You have to get used to the way they play. On top of that, you're a target from day one, so you get more than your fair share of attention from the opposition's hard men. You're also outside your comfort zone, so there's a lot for an overseas player to overcome.

Being out of your comfort zone is an interesting link into my second point about Jamie Lyon. There is perhaps no one in the current game who provides as good an example of player-power.

Don't get me wrong. I'm not saying that players gang together to force the club's hands. What I am saying is that nowadays players at the top of the game can and do exert their will to secure their interests. They have agents and managers who are on the lookout for opportunity. Rugby league is now an international business. It's not just about getting a trial with your local club, a chance to get in the team and building from there. Neither is it about a job for life, or even for a career. There are still players who dream of turning out for their local club, get the chance and then stay put for most of their careers. But increasingly players cherry-pick opportunities in Europe or Australia, in league or union. The international game in union is still bigger than its league counterpart. A player who feels he might achieve international selection in union might switch codes even though the day-to-day, bread-and-butter deal might not superficially look as good as what league can offer. I suppose this is something of a plea on my part for the game's administrators to continue their efforts to widen the base of rugby league and to ensure that the 2013 World Cup is used as a springboard to re-launch the international game to television audiences, in order to increase its profile.

To return to the players' angle, Jamie Lyon, for instance, decided he was retiring from big-time rugby league when he was 22. He was already an Australian international, and had already been the Kangaroos' youngest ever tourist at 19. But still he wasn't established in the national side when he was with Parramatta Eels.

But then Jamie Lyon was a country lad and found the pressure of city life and public spotlight tougher than many. When he was persuaded to stay on with his club for a whacking great fee, several players from older generations made comments about cynicism versus integrity. I doubt things were massively different in their day!

So, having eventually negotiated his way out of his Eels commitments, he was apparently destined for the relief of minor league football for a complete change. Then St Helens came up with another pot of cash for a two-season deal. You can't help feeling that either Jamie Lyon or his agent likes to dabble in playing hard to get!

After St Helens, he appeared to be heading back to his old club when a new possibility arose. He eventually joined Manley and has since gone on to win Grand Final honours with them.

In British-based rugby league this process began in the early 1980s with the star-studded Hull side that included no less a figure than Peter Sterling. We should remember, however, that the policy almost bankrupted the club. So in today's game, with player and agent power alongside club and management interests, all involved are learning new ways of operating. It's an aspect of the game that will develop fast in coming years.

But it's also worth remembering that reputations can be lost as well as won. In Jamie Lyon's case, he won his first cap as a teenager. He had a long wait until the Tri-Nations of 2006 for a return to the green and gold. He played one game only in the tournament and that was the 23-12 defeat by Great Britain. Like several other players in that side, it has taken him some time to shake off the consequences of defeat. No matter what the record looks like, don't ever think that any Australian ever takes things easy in an international game because the price of perceived failure can be very high indeed.

What about Jamie Lyon's try? Which should I choose? Should it show his blistering pace or perhaps his ability to cut through a defensive line into space?

Well, in the case of this centre with undeniable and amazing individual skill, I'm going to chose one that underlines the fact that rugby league is a team game. In an era of player power, expensive contracts and growing egos, a team only works if it combines its sum of individual skill via tactics into a single, efficient, effective unit. So the try is from the 2005 Good Friday fixture at the JJB.

There were over 25,000 crammed in for the game. Wigan had taken an early lead, but Saints were coming back. This try illustrates not only the essence of teamwork, but also how players in recent years have developed new handling skills and how they've come to anticipate and expect coordinated effort as part of the play.

It starts with a play-the-ball two metres inside the Wigan half on the Saints left. First receiver drives forward on a diagonal going left. Now in the older game, he might have put his head down, driven on and been happy with the extra five metres.

But here, when confronted by two defenders about to tackle, he turns and slips a pass straight back. He knows support is there.

The next receiver has a tackler immediately on him. He slips a lightning-quick pass to his right. This creates space and the next man makes ground, moving right and then straightening. At 15 metres out, he is centre-field when the cover tackler makes contact. Three Wigan players are near but not close enough. He offloads back and play then moves to the right. Again three Wigan players make the tackle but the player turns and offloads a one-handed flick, the pass slightly dollied.

The receiver has to wait. There's a tackler ready to pounce, arriving at the same time as the pass – so the receiver can't take the ball. Instead he does a two-handed push, like a union player in a lineout giving quick ball. Having drawn the cover, Saints now have three on the right to two defenders.

They are 18 metres out. The next receiver sprints diagonally to the corner and the cover follows. They are still ten metres from the line. Jamie Lyon moves inside from right centre as his teammate goes by. Then there's an inside one-handed reverse pass and Jamie Lyon receives.

The try needs scoring. He accelerates through the gap between two more cover defenders. The eye for the gap is perfect and he grounds the ball for the try.

In the move, nine Saints players touch the ball. There were seven passes, each of which was of a different style, as the ball went from left side on halfway to a try on the right wing. No less than eleven Wigan players made tackles or attempted tackles in the move, none of which stopped the ball. The handling skills made this look like basketball with contact!

Jamie Lyon missed the goal kick, by the way, and Wigan eventually won the game 22-20. In the era of international player power, it's still a team game.

19 – Ken Hirst

Having made an issue of how players and agents in the modern game often limit their involvement or commitment to the terms of the contract currently on the table, for my next score I want to feature a try by a player who was very much a one-club man. I also want to explore the idea that rugby league lacks personalities.

I have already stated my opinion that this isn't true, though few league players achieve celebrity status. If we understand 'personality' to mean a character living a full and varied life then rugby league is packed with them. Obviously, I want to contrast that idea with the word 'celebrity', which I think often refers to a marketing concept within the media. When we use the word personality in relation to sport, we often really mean celebrity in that we are celebrating not the person's current sporting performance, but their access to self-promotion.

If we look across different sports, we see that different conditions apply. Football, really, is out there on its own. It's a global sport and is number one in popularity almost everywhere except the United States. The US, of course, is very much a special case. It probably has more sporting celebrities than anywhere else, but in sports that elsewhere have limited spectator interest. How many baseball celebrities could you name? Now how many footballers come to mind? And how many of those are not British?

So if we ignore football as a special case, what is left? For spectator sports in Britain, we have rugby union and cricket. In some ways these sports are similar in that they both have long traditions, are just about nationwide and also operate within the old Commonwealth nations. But a point that is relevant to both is that, despite their loyal fan base and enduring interest, the majority of the games are played in front of very few spectators and with very little media interest. In the case of rugby union, apart from a handful of well-known sides in the recently established competitions, the sport is still largely amateur. Top of the table games and internationals attract big crowds, but the vast majority of games are played in front of sparsely populated stands. In cricket's case, the bread-and-butter games of the county championship are generally played in front of a few hundred spectators, no more. Later stages of knockout tournaments and test matches attract more attention. But it is perhaps fair to note that there is always greater interest in the score and result than in watching the game itself. Both sports, however, remain national in their presence.

Tennis, as a spectator sport, is probably a once-a-year event in the UK. At its highest level, tennis, like golf, consists of handfuls of players who travel the world repeatedly playing against one another. These are sports that have their dedicatees, for sure, but how many casual tennis fans have ever paid to watch a tennis tournament that was not an international tour event or Davis Cup? How many people have ever been to watch a tournament at their local tennis or golf clubs? It seems that these sports are mainly international and concentrate on the television audience. Players at the top of the tree receive substantial media coverage but a casual observer probably only recognises a few of the biggest names.

Now if you accept this picture then what price a game with strong regional but not national roots, whose players have in the past been almost exclusively home-grown and working-class, and whose venues have always been exclusively in the less than fashionable parts of the country? That rugby league has any media presence whatsoever given this scenario is a credit to the continued quality of its spectacle.

With the advent of Super League the establishment of various London clubs over the years, the creation of Catalan Dragons and Celtic Crusaders, plus the Murrayfield excursion, rugby league is, as always, trying to extend its penetration. As a game, rugby league always has been willing to change in order to bring this or another aspect of the game to the fore. In previous decades it experimented with a two-division structure to increase competition at the top. It chose to place limits on a team's possession.

Nowadays, Sky Sports has a loyal audience for Super League games. The games are often in the top ten most watched features on the channel. A recent National Rail Cup final – second division, if you like – sold out at Bloomfield Road, Blackpool. Nearly 9,000 people attended, despite the game being live on television. So the game itself is not at all unhealthy. And its continued willingness to innovate and change to increase its spread and appeal will surely see it make further progress.

So what about personalities? Well, if the game's penetration to other parts of the country were to succeed, if it were to become a national rather than a regional game, then media interest would increase and more of a celebrity culture might develop. But is this what we really mean by 'personality'?

The game has a long and rich history. There is a complete library of stories to be told about those who have been associated with it. My try selection was to be from 1980 onwards because I see the older game as not very relevant to the way it's played today. But there should always be space for good stories, because the people that populate those stories are interesting and, as such, are of permanent interest.

To illustrate such a story, I'm going to use a try from another Challenge Cup final, a try by a loyal, one-club player from the legendary water-splash final of 1968. I choose it not for the quality of the score, which frankly owes more to luck than good play. I choose it to illustrate that a good story will eventually become bigger than the events that generated it. For all kinds of reasons, and most of them not to do with the game, the 1968 final developed a celebrity all of its own. Now it was once suggested to Bill Shankly, the erstwhile manager of Liverpool, that football was only a game, it was not a matter of life and death. "It's far more important than that," is what he observed. When we look at the story surrounding Wembley 1968, we might demonstrate the accuracy of those remarks.

Wembley Cup finals are always great occasions. When rugby league was a purely regional affair, centred mainly on the mining areas of Yorkshire, Lancashire and Cumberland, the annual trek down south for the final was a great rugby league day out. Supporters of the participating sides obviously had pride of place, but the final's showcase status meant that people from literally all the other clubs also used to attend. It was not, therefore, a game that the organisers would want to call off at the last minute. In 1968 the 87,000 crowd awaited what promised to be a cracker of a final. Two great Yorkshire sides, close neighbours Wakefield Trinity and Leeds, had brought their local rivalry 200 miles south to Wembley. Leeds had completed a great season and had finished top of the table. They had beaten Wakefield twice in the campaign and were desperate to win one of the traditional big prizes to round off their season. But Wakefield were the side in form, with 16 successive victories behind them. Wakefield had just become League Champions under the old play-off system, beating Hull KR in the final the previous weekend, a game that was staged at Headingley, Leeds. The club had never before won both Championship and Cup in the same season. The game promised to be a cracker.

At about two o'clock that afternoon in May 1968, following a sunny start to the day, clouds thickened overhead and then burst. There was an almighty downpour, so heavy that the marching band on the pitch disappeared from view when it paced up to the other end of the field. It rained heavily for about half an hour, that's all. By the time the community singing, then an indispensable part of the Wembley occasion, was underway, there were just a few spots still falling. The crowd was less vocal that year when the traditionally white-suited Billy Scott-Coomber led them in *Ilkley Moor* and *She's A Lassie From Lancashire*, because everyone could see that the pitch was waterlogged. Discussion about whether the game could or should be played took precedence.

The Wembley pitch of that era was known to be heavy, even when only moist. That afternoon, its heavy soil with its slow drainage just couldn't cope with the volume of water, and there was effectively a pond where there should have been turf.

A small army of groundsmen appeared with garden forks, but it was obviously impossible even to make an impression on that amount of water. "They'll have to call it off," was said by most. It was surely inevitable. When, at about 2:45pm the public address clicked on, everyone expected the announcement. But all that came were team changes. Neil Fox, the great Wakefield centre, the game's record points scorer of all time, had been ruled out through an injury picked up in the championship final the previous week. Gert Coetzer, the South African left wing moved unexpectedly into the centre and Ken Hirst, himself a regular first teamer, took Coetzer's place on the wing. Wakefield fans knew the system because Neil had been absent through injury quite often that season and his brother, Don Fox, would take over the goal kicking responsibilities. But everyone was still surprised that the game was going ahead. "They can't possibly play rugby on that pitch," was unanimously agreed.

But they did, and the game was a complete farce. The ball was so slippery that neither team could handle it, neither hold nor pass nor catch it. It was lost in almost every tackle. A player under a heap of tacklers risked drowning as faces were pushed into the turf. Kicks went nowhere because in rugby league the ball has to bounce infield and that afternoon the ball couldn't bounce: it just stopped dead in the water. Even a fly-hack at a stationary ball wouldn't work because players kicked as much water as ball. Goal kickers couldn't place the ball – there were no kicking tees in those days – and the kickers slipped and slid during their run-ups. The scrums collapsed because no one could get a purchase on earth that had become saturated sponge. The pitch underneath the water churned up and great divots of turf appeared like molehills. The disappointment amongst the crowd at the lack of spectacle, however, soon became a passion, driven by the fantastic competition between the two teams.

Somehow, Wakefield got their noses ahead. But, in the second half, there was a crucial sequence of play. The ball had been dropped and Leeds advanced via a fly-kick. There were more contacts with the boot. The ball flew through the air toward the Leeds right, hit a puddle inside the Wakefield 25 and splashed to a halt.

There was a chase with players of both sides slipping and sliding. Gert Coetzer, the Wakefield stand-in centre, was adjudged by referee John Hebblethwaite to have impeded John Atkinson, the Leeds wing. The referee thus awarded a penalty try under the posts. At first, no one in the crowd understood what had happened. Most thought he had judged the ball kicked dead and had awarded a drop-out under the posts. Penalty tries are not a regular occurrence in the game. That try, plus the conversion, gave Leeds a lead. They celebrated even more when a kickable penalty made the score 11-7 with barely a tick left on the clock.

As the Wakefield team came up to centre-field to restart,

there was an announcement on the public address to say that the Lance Todd Trophy, awarded to the player with the greatest impact on the game, had been awarded to the Wakefield Trinity prop forward, Don Fox. He was on the losing side at the time but his contribution to the game had been nothing less than outstanding.

Trinity put the ball down at the centre and their forwards lined up. Don Fox foxed everyone by playing a quick, short kick-off to the opposite side. It took everyone by surprise except Ken Hirst on the wing who had planned the ploy with Don while they waited for the Leeds penalty.

The ball found a space and splashed to a dead stop in a puddle. Ken Hirst came infield, kept his feet and fly-kicked. Now both packs were on the other side of the field and were stranded. There were spaces. Ken followed up and made another contact with the ball. Surely he kicked it too hard. It would go over the dead-ball line. But the ball hit a puddle again and stopped just inches from the dead-ball line.

The Leeds defenders had to turn. Ken had momentum. There was a hand's width at the end. Ken's hand touched the ball and the try was given. The score was now 11-10 and the conversion was from just right of the posts. Don Fox had played an impeccable game and had already kicked two goals on this ridiculous pitch from difficult positions. When he placed the ball and stepped back, there probably wasn't a single person in the stadium predicting what happened next. The game was officially over. The Leeds players turned their backs, unable to watch. Don stepped back, advanced to kick, slipped, and missed it.

The man of the match sank to his knees and burst into tears. Every one of his teammates – except one – came to console him. Wakefield would not even have been in the game had it not been for his outstanding contribution. Eddie Waring's words, "He's missed it…the poor lad," have unfortunately entered the game's folklore.

I think that this event, perhaps for a whole generation, epitomises the difference between celebrity and personality. For years, even people who knew nothing at all about rugby league recognised this game. They could even remember the player's name and could certainly remember Eddie Waring's reaction. As 'the man who missed the kick', Don Fox received invitations to open supermarkets and attend public events. But he was far too proud a man, far too professional a player to milk his own and his team's misfortune.

It's when we get into the real issue of personality that we uncover a bigger story, and it's a story that could not have been invented. Its drama grew perhaps more intense as the years passed and events fell from public attention.

It was Ken Hirst's try that made the history. The try itself was nothing special, but its setting, its context and its stage were all heroic. Its consequences became historic. Ken was always Mister Nice Guy. He was a complete professional, not always a first team regular on the wing, but always a dependable player. He was scrupulously fair, had a spotless disciplinary record and was a loyal and faithful servant for his club. Had the try he scored been converted that afternoon in 1968, the Wakefield Trinity team would have completed a double that would have rendered their achievements automatically legendary. Ken is no longer with us unfortunately. He died in December 2008, his passing mourned by a loyal fan base who remembered his achievements for their club.

Unfortunately for Don Fox the label 'the man who missed the goal' endured. Call it celebrity, call it notoriety, it was a label he hated and tried to shake off. Don was one of the game's great players. He started his career as a scrum-half with Featherstone Rovers in a team alongside his elder brother Peter. Just five miles up the road their younger brother, Neil, having signed for Wakefield at 16, was making big headlines. The rivalry was always intense between the two sides and, at least on the pitch, also between the brothers.

They came from a rugby league hotspot, the then mining village of Sharlston, midway between Pontefract and Wakefield. Two of the greatest ever players, Jonathan Parkin who captained a Great Britain tour to Australia, and Neil Fox, the game's record points scorer of all time, came from the village. But there were many others, with names such as Bridges, Dooler, Mulaney and Smales being familiar to followers of the game.

But it was the three Fox brothers who epitomised the breadth of the game. Neil's prolific points scoring perhaps overshadows the fact that Don was arguably the best all-round player and Peter the better footballing brain, revealed in his successful coaching career. Don played for Great Britain just once, in 1963, after he had already made the transition to loose forward. It was a game against Australia at Headingley, a game that Great Britain won, with Don's contribution immense to one of the toughest encounters of all time.

But, as I've said, the man who missed the goal was a title that stuck. The phrase literally haunted him. Frankly, it destroyed his life, led to severe depression and illness. When its false celebrity eventually wore off, Don Fox, one of the game's outstanding players, was left a shell of a man and spent the last years of his life prematurely in care, but still visited by a loyal and selfless group of people associated with the game. When Don died in August 2008, his funeral in Sharlston church attracted large crowds of mourners, people who remembered him for his celebrity but also people who remembered him as a great player. But for one missed kick following a freak try in an idiotic game that should never have been played, he would surely have been a contender for one of the game's all time greats.

Now, if the story of the 1968 final thus far were not enough, there's yet another twist. The referee of that Cup Final wash-out was Mr John Hebblethwaite of York. Amongst the more irresponsible of the Wakefield Trinity supporters, there was such anger about his decision to award a penalty try that some people wrote him poison-pen letters. The media statements and intensity of the criticism that followed put Mr Hebblethwaite under real pressure. I'm not suggesting that this pressure was a determining factor. But when people are put under pressure, the effects are always cumulative. When Mr

Hebblethwaite died just over a year later, the circumstances that surrounded his death caused much debate. He committed suicide and there was talk of the aftermath of the 1968 game being a factor. For some years afterwards, it was always the rumour amongst Wakefield Trinity supporters that when a decision went against the team on the pitch, it was that day's referee paying the club back for what happened to Mr Hebblethwaite.

The reality of this story is far more poignant than any fiction. You could not have made this up! And it all stemmed from a try by Ken Hirst, fly-kicked across a pond in the last minute of a Cup final, to lose the game. The ultimate personality would seem to be the game itself.

20 – David Topliss

Rugby League Cup finals are great occasions. Northern fans have always complained about the long trip south to Wembley, but a more considered response always admits that the great stadium with its atmosphere and capital city status always gives the event more than the usual buzz. Great occasions only rarely generate truly great performances, however, because the tension of the event, alongside the fear of losing, often makes players hesitant. As a result, the Lance Todd Trophy, awarded to the final's man of the match since 1946, rarely goes to a member of the losing side. Usually a contribution that wins the game persuades the Rugby League Writers' Association members to award the Lance Todd to a try-scorer or play-maker from the winning side. There have been a few notable exceptions to this rule, one of which, David Topliss, the scorer of this try, I've already mentioned when describing Stuart Wright's 1979 try.

If Rugby League Cup finals remain great occasions, cup final replays are no less than historic in their significance. Since the Second World War there have been just two drawn finals. The first in 1954 saw Halifax and Warrington draw four points apiece at Wembley. The replay, at Odsal Stadium in Bradford, became a rugby league legend. Warrington eventually triumphed 8-4, with Gerry Helme scoring a late try for Warrington and winning the Cup. But it was not the three disallowed Halifax tries that elevated the replayed 1954 final into the game's history. It was the crowd. Officially, the attendance was 103,000, but it's been estimated that at least 20,000 more got in free when turnstiles couldn't cope with the rush and the mere 150 police on duty that evening couldn't prevent frustrated fans breaking from the queues to clamber over walls.

It was another 28 years, in 1982, before another final went to a replay. The game was a classic. Hull and Widnes had shared 28 points equally between them at Wembley and, because replayed finals were so rare, it took no less than 18 days to organise a re-match. It took place at Elland Road, Leeds on 19 May and over 41,000 fans attended. Hull triumphed 18-9 to lift the Challenge Cup for the first time since 1918. But what interests me about the game is not the result, or even the rarity of its replay. There was a try in the game that for me perfectly illustrates the role of stealth in rugby league and its ability, sometimes, to win matches. It was scored by

David Topliss, a truly great rugby league player, a man who, three seasons before, in 1979, had lifted the Lance Todd Trophy at Wembley as a loser, because his team Wakefield Trinity had been beaten by Widnes and Stuart Wright's kick-through try.

David Topliss joined Hull in 1981 at the age of 31. He'd played 13 years for Wakefield Trinity, a club he supported as a boy and to which he later returned as a coach. He was a man noted for his loyalty, dependability and honesty. It's said that he only left Wakefield because he understood that the £15,000 fee would stabilise the club's rocky finances.

Wakefield had been in the 1960s one of the game's top sides, but, during David's years at Belle Vue, Trinity never really achieved the heights. There's no doubt that he could have moved to a more successful club. There were plenty of offers, but throughout David expressed a clear wish to stay. He represented Great Britain, but would surely have had a more illustrious international career had he played in more high-profile games.

In the early 1980s, Hull FC were on the up and along with Hull KR formed my very first rugby league memories as a boy. They had a string of big-name signings in their ranks, several of them from Australia and New Zealand. So when David Topliss came to wear the number six jersey, he joined a potentially winning outfit. He'd always played with grace and style. His ability to ghost through defences using his tremendous acceleration was already legendary.

Now when teams have the strength and speed coupled with the tactics and the teamwork, what is it that can separate them when they compete? My answer to this is stealth. It needs a player who can do something special, something both individual and skilful that no one else on the field can conceive. If that player also has the ability to carry it off, then you have a match-winner. On many occasions, however, what we label as special is no more than professional, a tactic or manoeuvre that we'd expect from a skilled sportsman. On its own, without the strength and speed, the tactics and teamwork already matched, of course, individual brilliance might provide spectacle, but it doesn't necessarily win matches!

But sometimes a player does something that is truly unexpected, something that even surprises seasoned watchers of the game, and even the player himself! On 19 May 1982 a David Topliss try secured a Hull victory and, for me, perfectly illustrates how individual skill and vision can turn a game. Ray French was commentating that night. The game was gripping, tense and finely balanced. It could have gone either way. Ray had some advice for the Hull side, but, of course, only television viewers could hear it.

He says that Hull found weaknesses on the Widnes flanks in the first half. So, as Hull press forward late in the game, Ray French urges them to move the ball wide. Hull are centre-field near the 25. Charlie Stone runs straight and is tackled. There is a play-the-ball, and an inside pass, all down the middle. Keith Tyndall takes play to within five yards of the Widnes line. Hull have reached the sixth tackle of their phase. They play the ball left. David Topliss receives on the third pass and the odds are that he'll release towards the wing. But he has other ideas.

Displaying all the guile and skill that were his trademark, he steps off his left foot and cuts inside. The move makes a gap. That blistering pace off the near standing start propels him towards the line. Not only did Ray French not predict such a move, neither did the Widnes defence. It's but a split second later that the defenders react. They seem to converge on the Hull stand-off from all sides. But David instinctively curves his run into the only gap. Even when he gets to the line the try still needs scoring. There are two Widnes players making the tackle. A lesser footballing brain may have been held up, or rolled over short. But not David Topliss. The try, immediately left of the sticks, secures the game for Hull. It was a true match-winner, an example of stealth, the unconventional married to consummate skill. And it was this stealth that won the game, the individual skill of a player who knew both his talents and their limits.

'Toppo', as he was called, scored 270 tries in his career. In a rough, tough game he was a graceful gentleman. He won several Great Britain caps and was a member of the World Cup winning squad in 1972. He once captained the national team against Australia in 1982. In a game that needs all the personalities it can get, what a tragedy it is that David Topliss is no longer with us to grace its stage. He died from a heart attack in June 2008 at the age of 58 after collapsing in a five-a-side football match in Crofton, near Wakefield. It remains truly moving to read the tributes to him, posted by fellow players, fans, opponents and even foes. His try for Hull in 1982 is the perfect tribute to this great player.

21 – Robbie Paul

I'm proud of my achievements in rugby league. Though records are set to be broken, I doubt that any current or future English player will better my career try tally. To figure at number one on many lists of the greatest Challenge Cup final tries is more than gratifying. But in some ways I'm like a fisherman. It's always the ones that get away that are the best or the biggest, probably more so in the imagination than in reality.

Now, while I have a profound respect for many players, I've something less than respect for many others. But for me there's one guy who stands out, whatever the yardstick for comparison. In my eyes he has special status and my respect. But I'm also jealous of his achievements; well, one particular achievement at least. That player is Robbie Paul. And his achievement? Being the first player to score a Wembley hat-trick in a Challenge Cup final, of course, a feat I threatened to achieve twice, but never did – at least that's what the records say!

Robbie Paul is really the only player in rugby league history who I'm jealous of. There's one other whose achievement I envy, but I'm not jealous of as a player. So Robbie Paul is, in my eyes at least, in a class of his own. I scored 51 hat-tricks in Britain and one in Australia. It might even be a record. But none of them were in a Challenge Cup final.

Robbie and I have something in common. We both grew up in competition with older brothers. As a youngster in Hackney, I tried to compete with my older brother, but usually he won. I never got used to being second. As Robbie Paul says, it's the fear of losing that spurs you on to keep winning. The hurt of being on a losing side lasts longer than the joy of winning. So, again like Robbie, when I started to come in first, I wanted to stay there.

But when you do succeed, that's usually the start, not the end of the story. You have to do better next time round because everyone is gunning for you. The effect even has its own special name, the 'second season syndrome' or even 'sophomore slump' in the USA, because it's so common for a rookie's success to turn sour the following year. When I entered the game in 1987, I was *Man of Steel*. I was the first – and to this day the only – specialist winger to win the award. But that was not even my best season! I'm extremely proud of the fact that, even with everyone after me, I was top try-scorer for four consecutive seasons, my first four in the game, allowing me to record the fastest ever first 100 career tries in just 70 games. No one else had ever reached a ton in less than a hundred games. A Wembley hat-trick, however, eluded me.

Robbie grew up in New Zealand. The two-year gap between himself and his older brother, Henry, set the tone for Robbie's approach to sport. He says that Henry set the standards and he always followed. At least that's what Robbie says his brother would claim!

Robbie had a truly illustrious career in rugby league. He

joined Bradford Northern, later Bradford Bulls, in 1994. He captained the side in their all-conquering 2003 season and also led them to victory in the World Club Challenge against Penrith in 2004. He joined Huddersfield Giants in 2006 and then Salford in 2007. In 2006, Bradford staged a testimonial match for their loyal servant. But my jealousy of Robbie Paul stems from just one of his achievements, however: that Wembley hat-trick in 1996. The feat was on my list, but I never got to tick it off!

Wigan's run of Cup success came to an end in 1996. The club had lifted the trophy eight times on the trot and won 44 consecutive Challenge Cup ties when we went out to Salford. I know what Robbie Paul means when he talks of the pain of losing!

So that year the finalists were St Helens and Bradford. It proved to be an epic game and featured one of the greatest comebacks of all time. St Helens won the game, but their early dominance was threatened by a Bradford side that would just not lie down and be beaten. The final score was 40-32, but when Robbie Paul touched down for his third try, Bradford were within one score of Saints. It could have gone either way.

There's a play-the-ball in centre-field in the Bradford half. Graeme Bradley takes the pass as first receiver and drives on. It looks like he's been stopped, but somehow he slips the ball away to Karl Fairbank who makes his own drive to be tackled nine metres inside the Bradford half, dead-centre. Now that slipped pass could have played a part in Robbie Paul's try. For me, the St Helens players assumed the tackle on Bradley would be completed. When the ball came away, some players were taken by surprise.

Robbie Paul is first receiver from the re-start. He takes the ball on the burst, and it's some burst! There's a gap. He said later that it just opened up and he ran through it. The St Helens line is not fully formed. Perhaps it was the unexpected pass a moment earlier that had taken play several metres left of where they expected.

When Robbie Paul crosses halfway, he's already at top speed. Five metres on, there are two St Helens players ahead, two more in close attendance to his left and potential cover on both flanks.

What he does next is fascinating. He actually runs directly at one of the defenders – straight at him! Then, at only two metres range, he steps abruptly to his right. His closest tackler slips, wrong-footed. He's truly motoring by this stage and is through the gap.

But the fullback is ahead and has to be beaten. He takes a step to the left. Perhaps the fullback thinks this might be a dummy, a prelude to an all-out push to the right. But Robbie Paul steps left again, two left steps in two strides! He accelerates, rounds the fullback and then heads off to the right so he can score under the posts.

That was Robbie Paul's third try of the game. Purely on its own merits it was one of the greatest tries ever seen in a Cup final. It was the first ever hat-trick in a Wembley final and won him both the Lance Todd Trophy and a cheque for £10,000. It didn't win him a winner's medal, however.

A Wembley hat-trick was a real ambition of mine. I scored two tries in 1994 against Leeds and also two against Castleford in 1992. Actually, in that game I reckon I scored three. I thought I'd scored that elusive third try, but the referee disallowed it, judging I'd knocked-on. Now I reckon that in the game today, the different interpretation of the rules would have let that try stand. The two tries of mine that counted helped Wigan to beat Castleford 28-12 in 1992. When you get used to winning, defeat really does hurt. I know exactly what Robbie Paul means when he says that the pain of losing lasts longer than the joy of winning. And that's why I'm jealous of his achievement. For me, it was the one that got away.

22 – Jonathan Davies

I've said quite a lot over the years about the relationship between rugby league and rugby union. Obviously, I've played both codes. I remain grateful to rugby league in that it allowed me to pursue a career as a professional sportsman and taught me the discipline of professionalism. At the highest levels of rugby league, this was the essential aspect of the game that was often the difference between success and failure. There were many occasions during my years at Wigan when we came up against sides that, on the day, played as well or sometimes better than we did, matching us in almost every aspect of the game. Every aspect except one, that is. Often it was nothing more than our greater professionalism that took us through – our ability to do our job efficiently and consistently, despite the fact that we might not be at the very top of our game. When I switched codes back to rugby union, it was this professional approach that was so obviously lacking.

But on the other hand, rugby league is a simpler game than union. Don't get me wrong here. I'm not using 'simpler' to mean 'worse'. It's just different. The extra two players on a union side mean that there's always more cover defence and generally less space on the field. Add to that the difficulty of keeping possession, ruck and maul techniques, and lineouts to re-start play, and you have a much more complicated mix, over-complicated and over-technical, some might say, in rugby union.

Since rugby union became professional, the game, via its coaches and players, has improved its overall standards of performance, fitness, consistency and skill. At the highest level, rugby union can now achieve the same standards as league in these areas. But back in its amateur days, the transition from rugby union to rugby league was not just about learning the details of a different set of rules. It involved a complete shift on behalf of the player from part-time interest to full-time professionalism. If a player failed to make the transition, it was often a result of a lack of commitment rather than a lack of ability. And whoever makes the switch, it always takes time for the transition to take root, to become second nature.

Now such considerations applied when Jonathan Davies left rugby union to turn professional. When he switched to league it was a real bombshell. Though he began with

Neath, he was already a legend in Llanelli's colours and was a well-established international fly-half. He was so clearly the pick of the current bunch that his name would have been one of the first to be written into a British Lions team. So his switch created quite a stir in union circles.

It was also a matter of debate in league, with opinion initially divided as to whether he would be able to make the transition to the different demands in league. The rest, of course, is history.

Jonathan became a legend in league as well, but not, it has to be said, as a stand-off. In the end he played most of his league games at fullback but, perhaps paradoxically, it was his flair and speed in attacking play from that position for which he's remembered. The perfect illustration of this speed from deep is his try of 1994 against the Aussies. To this day I rib him about how I set this try up. I didn't, of course, but my role in the move does help to remind all of us that even moments of thoroughly individual brilliance happen on the back of sustained teamwork, a teamwork that is itself sustained by professionalism.

The Great Britain move starts from a scrum on our 20-metre line. Bobby Goulding picks up and goes left. He finds a gap and there's the break. He passes left to me and I cross the halfway line and make it as far as ten metres inside the Australian half before being brought to ground.

I went inside looking for an opening and space. In his commentary, Ray French suggested I should have stayed out wide because there was space on the flank. If I'd done that then Jonathan Davies's great try would never have been scored – hence my assist!

From the play-the-ball there are four passes to the right until the ball reaches Jonathan Davies who takes it near the halfway line. He sells a wicked dummy to his right and then makes a little step to straighten infield. Then he accelerates.

Many people associate my game with pure speed. But in fact I was not one of the fastest wingers. I used to race against Jonathan Davies in training and, though I generally finished in front, the margin between us was never great. In rugby you have to carry the ball; you don't often run in a straight line; you can rarely open up into a full sprint and you are always looking around for cover and support. Straight-line speed is only one of the factors involved in our game. It's how quickly you can cover the ground with the ball in your hands that counts. And, if you watch this try by Jonathan Davies, you'll see immediately that there have been few players in the game who were quicker than him.

When he breaks through in the 1994 game he leaves the defence for dead. His speed is decisive, but there is a fullback ahead and cover defenders in pursuit. Beating the fullback needs both guile and trickery. But a sidestep or jink allows the pursuers to gain ground. And they, of course, don't have to carry a ball. They just sprint.

Jonathan's solution to his dilemma is to find even more speed, to accelerate again from what looks like full pelt.

He makes the slightest of inside moves and then goes to the outside, perhaps critically and intentionally to Brett Mullins's left. There isn't a lot of space and the fullback's tackle comes in. But Jonathan's speed, momentum and no small measure of power carry him in at the corner. All right, I admit it, I didn't make that try, but Jonathan Davies's pure talent could only convert the score after good team play had created the position.

Jonathan Davies played for Widnes and Warrington in his rugby league career. He was Warrington's fullback in 1994 and this was his fourth try in a Great Britain shirt. It's true that skills do transfer across the rugby codes, but the playing context is different. Players who change codes have to adapt and those who don't can't make the transition. It takes hard work, dedication and not a little humility for someone who has been at the top in one code to start again and learn new skills. That's professionalism.

23 - 1988 Sydney

Getting off to a good start often sets the tone for a whole game. A team that gets ahead has more than points on the board. It instils confidence, makes you feel you're in control and suggests that things can stay that way.

It's even more important on big occasions. When your nerves are on edge and your confidence is lower than sky-high, getting on the scoreboard first is a real settling boost. It doesn't have to be spectacular, merely effective will do. So opening scores on great occasions often take on iconic status because of what they helped to set up.

And all of these things are true of my first try in the Third Test against Australia in 1988.

The context in which a try is scored is important and it's often especially important when it's teamwork that makes the score. You need the desire to win, to achieve, but you must also have the belief that anything is possible. These two things come together with confidence, and effective teamwork can build that confidence.

The 1988 Third Test between Australia and Great Britain in Sydney was a game that we weren't expected to win. We'd already lost the first two games and hence the series. The Australian press had written us off. For them, we were hardly even also-rans.

But we knew we could play. We knew that, as has so often been the case, we'd not yet given a good account of ourselves. And remember that the Third Test was a World Cup points scoring game. For both sides, there was much more than pride at stake.

It wasn't a spectacular try. I'd scored a real 'beaut' in Brisbane in the second test. It was a score that put me on the map in Australia and got me noticed. But it didn't win a game...

In my Sydney try, there's no particular stealth, no identifiable individual contribution that makes the score. Neither was there any real speed. It was a fairly short-range effort. But it was an opening score, brought about by effective, controlled teamwork and it did wonders for our confidence. We had it in our heads that the Aussies were better than us. But that opening score, because of when and how it was achieved, put self-belief alongside new confidence.

We'd started the game well and were in contention. Australia had threatened a couple of times after we had a touchdown ruled out following a high kick to the right corner. An Aussie had already crossed our line, but was held up on his back and couldn't ground.

We are near the Australian 20-metre line when Ellery Hanley, our captain, is tackled. He can't get up. He's incredibly slow to get to his feet and the crowd barracks him. So here we go again, I thought, under pressure and injuries mounting. That had been the pattern of the whole tour.

But then we put together some real teamwork. With Ellery Hanley needing treatment, we work the ball a drive closer the line. Hugh Waddell is dummy half. He feeds Andy Gregory on the left and he passes quickly to Kevin Ward. Andy follows his pass and, when Kevin Ward makes the half-break purely by using his strength, Andy is able to take the ball again on the loop. His next pass is to me, and it's absolutely spot on. It's again a quick release, but high, lobbed over the Australian defenders who have come into our line. It's unconventional, but hardly spectacular. More importantly it's perfectly weighted and right in my stride. I take the ball.

The rest looks easy. I have ten metres to run towards the

left corner to make the line. Rest assured, however, that they all need scoring. We've all seen players hesitate or fumble when presented with such chances. Take a split second too long and you'll be held up or bundled into touch. Well, in the event I get there for Great Britain's first points to break the early deadlock.

So why was that a great try? Well, we'd gone out onto the field that day already branded as losers. We'd been called no-hopers by the Aussie press from the start. We'd had a string of injuries and several replacements had flown out. Doing absolutely no injustice to those who played that day, the line-up was almost viewed as a second team. In some ways we had nothing to lose and everything to gain. If we'd lost that match by 20 points or even more, history would have judged that it had merely gone to form. But remember that the game was a World Cup qualifier in the days when teams won points in a mini-league to determine who would play off for the trophy. There was a prize on offer, for both sides.

As an outfit, we were resolved that day to do ourselves justice. We had faith in our own ability and believed that if we got the basics right we'd be in with a chance. But many Great Britain teams have thought that and gone out determined to succeed. And then Australia score and you're behind and, before you realise what's happened, you're beaten. Now it's hard enough playing against a team better than you, especially when you're professional enough to know it. It's even harder when they score first and their own confidence goes sky-high.

So, that 1988 afternoon in Sydney, our self-belief needed

a boost to confirm that the tactics were right and our teamwork could deliver. When Andy Gregory's looped pass found me, I knew immediately that the touchdown meant a lot more than just points on the board. In the context of the game, that try gave the whole team the confidence to carry the job through – and it worked. The match commentator, just as the try-scoring move gets going, says, "Let's see if they can put a string of passes together." He just gets to the end of the sentence before he answers, in a different tone of voice, "Yes, they do!" That's why this is a great try, because from then on, we also knew we could do it.

The try was also a milestone for me. I'd been in rugby league for only a year or so. I'd finished top of the table with Widnes and been selected as a Great Britain tourist. This was my third international try and I was about to be on a winning side against Australia. Most players in the game go through whole careers without ticking any of these boxes. The try wasn't spectacular, but for me it proved to be a momentous score.

24 & 25 – Leroy Rivett

Now I've already admitted that I'm jealous of Robbie Paul. I reckon all wingers who have a chance to play in a Challenge Cup final dream of scoring a hat-trick on the big occasion. I dreamt as well. I came close, but for me it was not to be.

But if I was jealous of Robbie Paul in 1996, three years later I was positively steaming about the achievement of Leroy Rivett in May 1999. Leroy is on record saying that he lay awake all night before the 1999 Challenge Cup Final. All he could do was imagine that he might score a hat-trick in what was to be the last final to be held at the old Wembley Stadium. In the 70 years of finals, only Robbie Paul had managed it, but Leroy had his dreams.

Well, he not only managed the hat-trick, he scored four and currently holds the record for the number of tries by one player in a Challenge Cup final. At the other end of fortune, I took a triple whammy that year, as things turned out. Not only did an opposition player live my dream of a Wembley hat-trick, but I finished on the losing side, and we went down to the highest score ever recorded by a winning team.

To be brutally honest, if Leroy Rivett's four tries had been scored in four different games, even four different Cup finals, then none of them would have made it into this selection. But he did score four in a final, and he does hold the record, so the feat alone is memorable. So often, iconic tries stick in the memory because of the setting and the context in which they were scored. Leroy Rivett's quartet fit perfectly into that mould. I'm going to include two of the four in this selection, numbers two and three.

The 1999 final was contested between Leeds and London Broncos. It was the Broncos' first and only final. Leeds had not won the Challenge Cup for 21 years. Shaun Edwards and myself were in the Broncos side that year. I moved there from Wigan in 1996 and Shaun followed a year later. Our team was led out onto the pitch that May afternoon by club chairman Richard Branson. There was a lot at stake for both sides. But the fact that the Broncos had already become part of the rugby league landscape, despite being based in the south, speaks volumes for the hard work and dedication amongst everyone involved with the club. I was 33 years old by then and often didn't play full games. I did, however, get my own personal dream start.

I opened the scoring with something of a freak try. But it still needed scoring! John Timu, the New Zealand centre, tried to find some space behind the Leeds defensive line with a grubber kick along the left touchline. It was intended for me to chase. He misdirected the kick and it went straight to a Leeds player. But the ball had some pace and ricocheted off the player's shins. It went straight to me. Having anticipated the kick, my marker was wrong-footed. I did one of my trademark jinks inside followed by a sprint to the corner. It could so easily have been my day!

In fact, the Broncos were ten points ahead in no time at all. At half time the score was 12-10 to Leeds and, really, there was nothing at all between the teams until the game reached the last quarter. Then, it has to be said, we tired and Leeds' greater fitness and professionalism prevailed. I went off with a dead leg at half-time. It's just another case of what might have been…

Leroy Rivett scored one of the Leeds tries in the first half. It was a perfectly good try, a winger's try, but not remarkable. The looped pass that found the Leeds winger went over my head. I was tempted to intercept. I did get fingertips to the ball, but I couldn't deflect it enough to prevent it reaching Leroy Rivett who was basically behind me. The winger gathered while I was still coming down from my stretch and he ran in from ten metres. His second try, however, was a different matter. I include it in this *50 Of The Best* as an example of a try created by teamwork.

It was a classic rugby league move. From a set piece, there's a break by a half-back. A long diagonal run gains ground and creates an attacking position. There's a quick drive and then a fantastically quick switch to the other side of the field. A long miss-pass creates an overlap and Leroy Rivett runs in another winger's score in the right corner. It was Ryan Sheridan who took the ball away from the scrum on the Leeds 30-metre line, right side. He ran 70 metres and was tackled just five metres short near the left touchline. The next drive finished three metres short and then the ball went right the entire width of the field. The overlap that this slick and fast passing created was enough. This was superb teamwork. The try was quite unstoppable and Leroy Rivett ran in at the right corner.

After that score, the floodgates opened. The Broncos were tiring. This was illustrated when Karle Hammond's pass, aimed for Tulsen Tollett, provided easy meat for an interception. We were just ten metres from the Leeds line, but had thrown everything forward. When Leroy Rivett took the ball and raced no less than 90 metres to score, the cover defence never had a chance.

I've said elsewhere that interception tries are rarely memorable. The defence is on the wrong foot. If the ball is taken cleanly, the attacker has a head start while the defence has to check and turn. Frankly, if this try had not been the third of a Wembley hat-trick, it would not feature in my fifty. But it was a Wembley hat-trick, and I never achieved one!

Leroy scored a fourth late on to complete his record-breaking quartet. His dream had come true. For me, it was time to move on again. The following year I went to Salford, the club where I played my final two seasons in the game.

I did achieve many of my goals: 500 tries and the greatest ever try in a Challenge Cup final amongst them. The Wembley hat-trick eluded me. That's the way life goes sometimes. Just ask Leroy Rivett. At the time, pundits were predicting a bright future for the winger, including international honours. But it never really happened for him. I might be jealous of this one achievement of his, but I bet the boot's on the other foot from his standpoint.

26 – Phil Ford

Rugby league families have featured quite a lot in my *50 Of The Best*. And not all of them have hailed from the game's heartland. There are far too many to list, but a few names may jog some memories.

In recent times there have been Sinfields, Pryces, Cunninghams, Burgesses, Gardeners and Gleesons in the game. A few years ago there were two brothers named Paul that I recall, and two others called Rayne whose careers were not quite as illustrious as the Pauls'. There have been Iros and Leuluais. In my days at Widnes we had Hulmes and O'Neills. Brian Bevan's brother played the game for a while. And the name Fox comes up repeatedly. Of the three Foxes, two are in the Rugby League Roll of Honour. The youngest is the highest point scorer ever, the eldest coached Great Britain while the one in the middle, definitely for the wrong reason, is one rugby league player whose name even those outside the game can remember.

In the Hull side of the 1960s, there were no less than three sets of brothers for a while. The Drakes were twins. There were two Whiteleys, one of them, Johnny, arguably one of the best loose forwards in the history of the game. And I've already described the great Clive Sullivan, but don't forget that his brother Brian also had a spell with the club.

Fathers and sons are equally well represented in the game's history. Here's just a few names that come to mind – Agar, Burgess (again!), Newlove, Batten (twice!), George, Risman to name but a few. The Mylers are more of a dynasty! And there's also Sullivan again, of course, Anthony being Clive's son.

But let's now use the Sullivan model of brothers and a son, but exemplified by a different family and brought forward 20 years to illustrate how the sport of rugby was at the start of a period of change. Like the Sullivans from Cardiff, and brought up on rugby union, were the Fords. Phil Ford is my featured try scorer, but let's look at the rest of the family. Brother Steve was also a winger. He played rugby union for Cardiff and was capped eight times for Wales. It's reported that he was also suspended for a time by the Welsh Rugby Union for taking a trial with Leeds. Now, that was 20 years ago, about the time that I entered rugby league. Things had moved on by 1990. But when I switched to league in 1987, it was definitely a one-way ticket. Steve Ford just managed to book his return trip and had a great career in rugby union. He also had a son named Luke, and he's already represented Wales at the Under-20 level. In his own words, he's more like his uncle Phil: laid-back.

The Fords are a real cross-code rugby family because when Phil retired from a rugby league career with Warrington, Wigan, Bradford, Leeds and Salford, he went back to Wales and took up rugby union again. If you search the internet for 'Phil Ford's try', you'll find one he scored for Pontyprydd, not Great Britain.

Phil Ford's nickname was *The Rubber Man*. It was a pretty tough, durable sort of rubber! He'd been vulcanised at some point, no doubt. The title came from his almost relaxed but deceptively quick style of running, his apparent meanders that so often proved decisively direct. And there is no better illustration of this style than – what else could I pick? – the 1988 try for Great Britain against Australia in Sydney.

It's the first half. We have our noses ahead by virtue of my own try on the left. We have a penalty that Paul Loughlin puts into touch on the right, 30 metres from the line. Paul Hulme restarts and Hugh Waddell drives up to the 22-metre line. Paul Hulme is dummy half and passes left to Andy Gregory, who passes left again to Kevin Ward. He turns in the tackle and offloads a short ball to

Mike Gregory. He sets off back to the right and makes ground before passing left to Paul Hulme. He turns into his tackle and offloads, but the pass is lobbed and speculative. It goes to ground. We get a kind bounce that Andy Gregory gratefully collects almost in stride. There's a bit of luck here. That ball could have bounced anywhere. It would have been easy to knock on.

Andy Gregory is back on the 22-metre line, centre-field. He runs sideways to his left – the very thing the Australian press criticised him for on the previous tour! He's darting, elusive. He steps right and left to avoid Wayne Pearce. He goes further left and now has Wally Lewis and Gary Jack ahead. The fullback gets a hold, but Andy Gregory turns and offloads again. That's the third offload in this move! Again the pass isn't perfect, but it's safe and in Phil Ford's hands.

And again we're back on the 22-metre line. Phil Ford reverses the move and sets off to his right. It seems permanently cross-field until he steps off his right foot to straighten. Then the pace kicks in. At 15 metres out he steps to the right, and then right again, so more cross-field. A sharp left then takes him past a defender. "He's a stepper, Ford!" says the match commentator.

And now there's a gap. There are four Australian defenders in attention, but there's a diagonal line straight through them and Phil Ford takes it. None of them gets a hand on him. When he grounds the ball just to the right of the posts, all Peter Sterling and Tony Currie can do is help him down.

I've now included three of Great Britain's tries from that game in my *50 Of The Best*. My own first try wasn't spectacular, but scoring it through such sound teamwork set us up with the confidence we needed to go on and win. Henderson Gill's try was a spectacular length-of-the-field effort. Phil Ford's try, however, displays another side of the game: sustained pressure created by coordinated and prolonged teamwork that is then converted into a score by individual brilliance. Later, I'll also feature Mike Gregory's try in the same game, another length-of-the-field spectacular.

But in many ways Phil Ford's try is the best of the four. Take into account the sustained way that the team pressed to create the chance. Great Britain probed for a gap along the 22-metre line, prying for an opening. And our tactic of keeping the ball alive by using the offload in the tackle came off. In the final move, there were no less than six passes. It was set up by a platform of strength and teamwork, where each player did his job, but also had the flair to spot a gap. Then, in the end, it was scored with pure individual brilliance and considerable speed.

I doubt any other player in the last 30 years could have scored that try. It's the perfect example of *The Rubber Man's* talent, but also shows how direct the effect could be.

27 – Joe Lydon

Though I've said that interception tries are rarely memorable, there's no denying the quality of Joe Lydon's score for Widnes in the 1984 Challenge Cup

Final. It was not really an interception try, but it did come from a breakdown of play, meaning that the opposition, Wigan that day, were very much on the wrong foot when the ball was lost. But what makes Joe Lydon's try special is one thing and one thing alone – speed.

Joe Lydon is one of the most famous and most accomplished rugby league players of all time. He won 30 caps for Great Britain and made the record books as the first player to break the £100,000 transfer barrier when he moved from Widnes to Wigan in 1986. He stayed at Wigan until 1994, scoring 90 tries and 309 goals in 292 games with the club. But it was Widnes where Joe's professional career began. And it was with Widnes, against Wigan, in 1984 that he scored perhaps his most memorable try.

Wigan are on the attack. Widnes are in front, but there's enough left in the game for the result to be in doubt. There's an attempted chip kick over the Widnes defence, but it is too close to the defensive line. The ball finds a Widnes hand. There's a stroke of luck as this first pair of hands can only parry. A second pair of hands clean up and feed a pass left, while actually falling in a tackle, to Les Gorley. He drives on, draws the defender and feeds a perfectly-timed pass to Joe Lydon, playing left centre that day, to put him completely in the clear.

Throughout my *50 Of The Best*, I've said that speed is one of the essential elements of a rugby league player. Nothing illustrates this better than Joe Lydon's 70-metre sprint to score in 1984. Not only did no Wigan player lay a hand on him but there was no one on the pitch that was in the same race. A clean pair of heels is the expression we often use. Well, these heels positively shone.

Widnes took advantage of a mistake and finished clinically. The kick that was parried was a poor effort, but in what seems only the blink of an eye, Widnes have collected the ball, created their own opportunity and converted it into a score. That, put simply, was the rugby league equivalent of a knockout punch!

Joe Lydon's 1984 try was memorable for its speed, pure and simple. The two tries he scored that day were enough to win him the Lance Todd Trophy. But don't for one minute think that these skills were purely about finishing. Four years later, it was Joe Lydon's speed again that proved decisive. It was in a Wigan shirt in 1988 that, as we've already seen, he broke clear to set up Ellery Hanley's try against Halifax.

Now I've not dwelt on my description of Joe's try or the game. That's because I want to use this entry in my *50 Of The Best* to highlight other aspects of Joe's involvement with rugby. The casual follower of the game may not be aware that Joe Lydon's association with the game has spanned his entire life.

His first appearance at Wembley was as an eleven-year-old in a curtain-raiser before the 1975 Challenge Cup Final. Then, in a professional career with Widnes, Wigan and Sydney City Roosters, he won just about everything in the game several times over.

But on retiring from the field of play, Joe has not only

continued his involvement with rugby, he's taken it to new heights. Just look at some of the things he's done. He was Director of Wigan Warriors from 1994 to 1996 and the Performance Director for the Rugby Football League until 2000. He then switched codes to coach the England rugby union Under-19 side, and followed that in 2001 with an appointment as Sevens head coach. In 2004 he was backs coach for the England rugby union side. He is currently head of Rugby Performance and Development for the Welsh Rugby Union and, on top of all that, is still involved with Wigan.

Joe Lydon's career reminds us of two things The first is that what we see on the pitch is often the product of long hours of dedicated work to develop skills and identify tactics. Without tactics and teamwork, at the highest levels of the game you don't have a price, and these qualities have to be taught and learned. Secondly, we must always be aware that without dedicated people who work to develop the game at every level, then the pinnacle that we see on television or on a Super League pitch simply would not exist. We've returned again to the theme of professionalism in its widest sense.

28 & 29 – Shaun Edwards

To say that Shaun Edwards is one of the game's greats is an understatement. He's achieved so many honours over the years that it's impossible and unnecessary to list them. Nowadays he's nothing less than a household name, but rest assured there's still a lot to come from this Wigan lad.

I suppose that this last phrase is a crucial one. In my autobiography I made the point that if Shaun had been born outside rugby league's heartland, he would probably have become a world-famous rugby union player. After all, he captained England schoolboy teams in both codes.

Shaun is now somebody I would describe as a good friend and confidant, but it wasn't always like that, largely due to a throwaway comment I made during a Challenge Cup Final telecast.

He's a man who helped me through some low times at Wigan. At about the same time that someone called Henry Paul poked me in the eye, his sound advice of "If it ain't broken don't fix it, lad" really helped. He followed up with "Just get stuck in!" It might sound simple, but it was just what I needed, as I was totally overcomplicating things and taking myself far too seriously. This was the piece of advice that put me back on track, helped me keep my place in that great Wigan side and led me to Wembley in 1994, and the rest, as they say, is history.

When Shaun signed for Wigan as a teenager for that world-shattering £35,000 fee in 1983, he still had everything to do in the game. But didn't he do it! And there is one of Shaun's achievements that's unique for a professional rugby league player and, in many ways, it hasn't received the recognition it deserves. He became the first rugby league player to hold aloft a significant rugby union trophy when he lifted the 1996 Middlesex Sevens for Wigan. We were a professional league outfit.

We went to the very home of rugby union, played to our strengths and were able to control games in a code we didn't practise. And Shaun led us to that win.

It would be easy to string together a list of superlatives to describe Shaun's career. It would also be pointless, because everything has already been said. What I want to focus on is an aspect of the game that for me Shaun Edwards exemplifies, and that is support, in all its meanings.

I will always remember how Shaun and Ellery Hanley in particular used to become completely focused on a game and the job that lay ahead. Laughing and joking stopped and pure, simple professionalism took over. In many ways I learned my own professional approach from these two great players.

But what he also taught me was how to prioritise. I wanted to score a try or set one up every time I had the ball. I used to get frustrated with myself and others when things didn't work. But it was Shaun who took me to one side and reminded me that patience and hard work would pay off in the end. If you try to force every play, he told me, you get frustrated. Concentrate on taking the chances that come along. It was sound advice.

I suppose that this advice is also at the core of the point I want to make about Shaun's game. What he gave me at Wigan was assistance and support, and this is precisely what Shaun gave all his teammates, year in, year out on the pitch. Shaun was never the quickest player, though you would never think so when you recollect how many times he outpaced defenders to score. But the key with Shaun was support. It was being available, in the right place at the right time. He could only deliver with his support play because of his incredible fitness. He could run up and down the middle all day, and that fitness was the product of nothing more nor less than hard work and dedication.

As I said in my autobiography, rugby league is a simple game. I repeat that this does not belittle it in any way. Basically, we all know the team that scores the most points wins the game. To score you first have to make chances and then you have to take them. There are occasions when individual brilliance wins matches. But usually the side with the better organisation, more coordinated teamwork, and superior professionalism will win. In rugby league it takes a break to create space and opportunity, but – apart from individual brilliance so rare that people write books about it! – it's teamwork that counts and the key element in that teamwork is support. And when it came to supporting the player on the break, Shaun Edwards was quite simply in a class of his own.

I've chosen two tries to illustrate this. Neither is particularly spectacular. But, when you read the descriptions or look at the videos, just think of how many times you've seen Shaun Edwards do this. And, if you're going to remember his playing days, just look at his record!

So for me the important thing about these tries – and the reason I've included them – is what they symbolise. They exemplify support play at its best. When I see a player like Richie Myler or Danny Maguire run that inside support line in the modern game, it makes me smile and I remind myself that I used to do that and I learned it off Gizmo, aka Shaun Edwards.

The first try is from the 1985 Challenge Cup Final at Wembley against Hull, the one that many people think Wigan would have lost if the game had lasted another five minutes. Shaun was wearing the fullback's shirt that day because Brett Kenny was at stand-off, facing his club and country partner Peter Sterling who was wearing the Hull number seven. Shaun was to develop quite a stormy relationship with Brett Kenny, all stemming from his own utter commitment and professionalism and his complete intolerance of anything less in others. In this particular try, however, they worked together.

There's a scrum ten metres inside the Hull half, centre-field. Mike Ford feeds Kenny to the right and then follows the pass to loop around his half-back teammate. Kenny turns as if to slip a return ball, but dummies. The effect of Ford's dummy-run followed by Kenny's dummy is that the Hull stand-off has had to move to his right to cover the Wigan scrum-half's run. This means that Peter Sterling has had to come from the scrum to challenge Kenny. Now you would have thought that Peter Sterling would know everything there was to know about Brett Kenny's play!

Well, perhaps he does, but the slight hesitation brought by the dummy plus the extra time that the dummy-run created produce a delay in Sterling's tackle. He has Brett Kenny's leg, but low down and the Wigan man gets free.

There's the break. There's the chance! But it will only come to something if there's support.

Kenny is in space. He goes straight down the middle at full pelt. He has fullback Gary Kemble ahead. But he doesn't jink or sidestep or indeed take any risk whatsoever. Why? Because to his right in perfect position he has the Wigan fullback, Shaun Edwards, waiting to receive. Now how did Shaun get into that position?

The pass goes right and Shaun takes. Ray French on the match commentary asks, "Has he got the legs for the line?" He has answered almost before the sentence is complete: "Yes, he has," because Shaun is already grounding the ball unopposed. It's copybook stuff. A break creates an opportunity. You have a chance of scoring if you support it. It's not rocket science. It's so simple. But wait a minute. If it was that simple, wouldn't everyone be doing it all the time? Now you know why it makes me smile when I see another player from a new generation cotton on.

Now it's one thing to be there and available, pulling out all the stops, on the big occasion when everyone is motivated. But how about doing it week in, week out consistently well to stay ahead of the chaser?

Well, here's a second try of Shaun's. It's perhaps less spectacular than the Wembley effort, but note the similarity of the position.

This one is in 1988. It's a Lancashire Cup final against

Salford, a game that Wigan shaded 22-17. When you watch the video, one thing that stands out is the state of the pitch. It's not quite a mud bath, but it's not far off. You might even find it hard to identify particular players. Well, Shaun Edwards is one of the players with a muddy shirt.

The one that doesn't have a muddy shirt, Wigan substitute number fifteen, receives from a play-the-ball ten metres inside the Wigan half, right of centre. He drives to centre-field and is half-stopped, but can turn and offload. The pass goes back to the right. The big fellow has drawn in defenders and the receiver has space to forge a break.

But the break has to be on the diagonal towards the right touchline. It's a decisive break, but the cover is coming across. There are a couple of players in muddy shirts to the left of the player in possession. Who are they? Well, one is Shaun Edwards and he's in perfect position.

But the Salford cover is almost in line with the pass. The best option is to kick. And so, just before the tacklers snuff out the break, there's a perfect cross-field kick that lands centre-field.

Shaun was already in the perfect supporting position. Now he takes ten metres off the defenders in a 35-metre charge to the bouncing ball. He helps it along with a tap from the boot and, though he has to wait for the bounce, he touches down ahead of the tackler under the posts.

These are two opportunities taken, two amongst the

literally hundreds that Shaun took or assisted over the years. He played over 450 games for Wigan and his record is second to none. As a coach he's still motivating players by supporting them, whether that be with Wasps, the Welsh National Rugby Union team, or the British Lions. He's still fit by the way, but I reckon he's got a bit stout recently! Only joking, Gizmo.

30 – Jason Robinson

I suppose I ought to be jealous of Jason Robinson. In some ways I am. But we're players of different eras, products of our time. Jason's achievements in rugby union are now legendary. But these were things that were not even conceivable, let alone possible, when I was at my peak. You can't be jealous of the impossible. And in terms of rugby league, Jason and I shared similar honours.

Like me, Jason was a winger. We both played for Wigan, of course, on opposite flanks. I played 145 games for a highly successful Widnes side before joining the Warriors, whereas Jason turned out just 27 times for lowly Hunslet in a single season before hitting the big time. While I had already won most things in the game before I joined Wigan, including a World Club Challenge, Jason was very much a rookie when he arrived, still waiting to get his first winner's medal.

But Jason's record is nothing less than exceptional. With Wigan he lifted every trophy in the game. And then, with Sale Sharks and England rugby union, he also won the Guinness Premiership, a Grand Slam and a World Cup, as well as touring with the British Lions. In the future, I'm sure that Jason will be seen as the first rugby player of a new era for both codes. I've remarked on this already when describing Brian Carney's career, but though he was not the first to make the transition, Jason was the player who achieved success at every level in both games. The rule changes, of course, came just too late for me.

Jason was born and raised in Hunslet, south Leeds. Now Leeds is a rather divided city. The north, generally, is leafy and middle-class, whereas the south is solidly working-class, industrialised and, in parts, less than pretty. Leeds used to boast three rugby league clubs, as well as rugby union sides. The always fashionable Leeds still has its headquarters in the equally fashionable north of the city at Headingley, an area with its rugby union and cricket links. The test-match cricket ground actually adjoins Headingley Stadium, now home of the Leeds Rhinos, of course. Bramley, 'The Villagers', on the other hand, were always based on the western edge of the city, in a class no-man's-land. Barley Mow and later McLaren's Field were their home territory. The club's sole honour of note was the BBC2 Floodlit Trophy of 1973. They happened to beat Widnes at Naughton Park. Times have changed since then.

Hunslet, however, were in days gone by a very famous club. Their history is long. One of the game's legendary names, Billy Batten, signed for the club as a 17-year-old and in the 1907-08 season helped his club to do 'the all four cups', the legendary feat that was accomplished by only three teams in the 80 years or so that the trophies were contested, and no one managed it post-war. Wakefield Trinity were perhaps the closest in 1962. They already held three cups when they were defeated by Huddersfield in the championship final at Odsal, having already defeated the same team the week before at Wembley to win the Challenge Cup. So Hunslet's name is up there with the greats. At least it was. They had a strong side and a strong tradition. They lost at Wembley to Wigan in 1965 – and only just lost! – but a few years later the club was defunct. Their Parkside home in south Leeds, amongst the railways, the gas works and industrial areas of the city, was set alight by vandals.

By the time Jason Robinson graduated through the ranks in his home club, Hunslet were true minnows, their tradition of greatness utterly lost. They'd played at several different grounds, had folded, been re-launched by one of Hunslet's great servants, Geoff Gunney, had a new name a couple of times and had won nothing. But Hunslet was Jason Robinson's club and it was for them that he signed in 1991. It didn't take long for the rich and powerful to notice his talents.

An offer came from Leeds, but Jason refused to consider it because he wanted to honour his agreement with Hunslet. But then at the end of the season a better offer came in, from Wigan. So in 1992, Jason Robinson was, like me, a Wigan man.

Jason has scored some wonderful tries for all the teams he's played for. But the one I've chosen for my *50 Of The Best* is here more for its significance than its individual brilliance. Jason has scored more spectacular tries than this, especially in his rugby union days, but for me this try, once scored, could never be bettered in his career. The reason? Its setting and its circumstance were unique, and remain so to this day, fifteen years after it was scored.

Rugby league's World Club Challenge, rather like its World Cup, has a chequered history. It started in 1976. There was a second game in 1987, but it really wasn't properly organised and official until 1989, when Widnes played Canberra and I was on the winning side!

It then became a regular fixture until the mid-1990s, when Australia's Super League war disrupted everyone's plans. The game was not contested again until 1997, but since then it's been staged every year. Though there has been criticism of the fixture based on the fact that it's generally played in Britain in the Aussie off-season. But as far as I can see if a team wants to take the game seriously and win it, then they can. After all, we've all been professionals for many years now and professionals don't opt out. Rest assured, however, in 1994, when Wigan faced the Brisbane Broncos in Queensland, the Aussie side took the game seriously and wanted to win. In the history of the World Club Challenge, only one English team has ever lifted the trophy on Australian soil. And that team was Wigan in 1994 and it was Jason Robinson's second-half try that put the seal on the game.

It was a real Jason Robinson special. His speed and particularly his acceleration were his greatest assets. He could also sidestep a bit! And all these three talents he displayed in this try, along with a fourth – a killer instinct. When Jason Robinson saw a chance, he gave it all he had.

Wigan led by virtue of two first-half tries from Denis Betts and Barrie-Jon Mather. That second try could easily have been mine, but the centre used me as a decoy and went in himself to Wendell Sailor's left. Had he passed inside to me, I could have gone under the posts. He also had Jason to his right, but Jason could only have gone in at the corner. I was the better option. And we do always say that good centre play is always unselfish...

Then Brisbane fought back. The Aussie outfit was not taking this game lightly. They wanted to win and the 57,000 Queenslanders in the stadium that night were baying for our blood.

But we were a weakened side. Both of our regular props were out injured and Kelvin Skerrett and Andy Platt were not players that any team – even Wigan! – could afford to lose. We also lost Martin Dermott in the first half. It's funny how the memory of certain feelings can stay with you for the whole of your life like passing your driving test or failing exams. Shaun Edwards and I still joke to this day about the feeling of dread we felt when we woke up that morning. We were up against the best team in the world and were going to get annihilated. We both learned that day how big a motivating factor fear can be. Not fear of failure, but fear of international embarrassment!

So, getting our noses in front definitely helped calm the nerves. A large part of the second half was devoted to consolidation via solid defensive work, but a piece of brilliant opportunism helped us on our way. It came from Jason Robinson. It was purely his try. No other Wigan player touched the ball. If he had an assist, it was from the backing up of substitute Martin Hall. But in the end his only role was to be the receiver of a dummy. Well actually, it was Wendell Sailor who took the dummy.

It's the second half. Brisbane Broncos number 13 Julian O'Neill is tackled by Wigan centre Sam Panapa ten metres inside the Broncos half. O'Neill slips the ball inside from the tackle. It's a perfectly good pass, at a catchable height, in the receiver's stride and nicely weighted. The Broncos number two Michael Hancock, who later became my teammate at Salford, is in perfect position but, for some reason, spills the ball. It's one of those aspects of the game that you can't plan or predict. Sometimes people make mistakes, sometimes they don't. Sometimes teams merely take advantage of mistakes, taking possession or securing a changeover or a head and feed scrum. Sometimes, however, mistakes are punished, and when they are, it's a double whammy for the team on the end of the punch. They themselves have lost a position, given it away on the cheap, and then they have been punished by a decisive move against them, a move whose possibility they themselves presented. Because of that psychological blow, it could be that, without Jason Robinson's try, the Brisbane Broncos might have come back to win.

When Hancock drops the ball he misses the real opportunity of a defence-splitting break. The ball goes to ground. Jason's lightning reflexes react and he gets a toe to the bouncing ball. He controls it. Even on the video footage you have to be quick to see what happened. That little toe contact made the score!

Hancock has his arms around Jason at this point. But because our man has played the ball with his foot, the Broncos man can't tackle. He's afraid of conceding the penalty. In the event, that would have been the better option. So he lets go and Jason Robinson picks up, and is immediately deadly.

Now speed and acceleration from a standing start are special talents. I've already noted this in the case of David Topliss. David's flat-out speed was nothing special, but the time it took him to achieve it was. Jason Robinson had the same talent, only much more of it.

He sets off slightly to his left. Willie Carne gets a hand on him, but it's less than a half-tackle. And Jason is past him. He speeds over the Broncos' 40-metre line, then straightens and opens up to full speed. A gap opens and he takes it. No one puts even a finger on him.

Ahead there's Wendell Sailor to beat. The Broncos' winger is miscast that evening as a fullback. And Jason Robinson has support to his left in the form of substitute Martin Hall.

Jason dummies to his left and then goes right, just a little, just enough. Sailor gets hands on our man but he's over for the score.

It was a try that summed up Jason Robinson's approach to the game. It was decisive, direct and destructive – at least for the opposition. I say it won the game for us. And so Wigan lifted the World Club Challenge on Aussie soil, to this day the only time it's been done.

As I said earlier, I'm sure that Jason Robinson has scored better, more spectacular tries than this. But when the score secures something that remains wholly unique, its status is surely iconic.

31 – Wayne Pearce

Sometimes tries achieve iconic status because of what they symbolise. In those cases, it may be that the try itself is not so memorable. Wayne Pearce's 1982 try, however, was a spectacular effort, but what it illustrated was far more important.

It was October 1982. The teams for the First Test between the Australian tourists and Great Britain took the field at Boothferry Park, Hull in front of almost 27,000 spectators. The Kangaroos' tour had started well with a victory against Hull KR and, by the time they took the field in Hull for the second time, they'd notched up six straight wins. The major talking point at the time was the Australians' decision not to play the established half-back pairing of Steve Mortimer and Wally Lewis and to field the younger pairing of Peter Stirling and Brett Kenny. Wally Lewis was vice-captain of the tour party and not even in the side!

Australia had impressed, but against five club sides and then a Wales team that was very much an experiment. Now they were up against a Great Britain side and home expectations were high. It's worth remembering that in 1982 it was just ten years since Great Britain had last won the World Cup. It might be hard for some younger supporters of the game today to imagine the expectation that surrounded that First Test match. Australia were the dominant international side in the game, but in 1982 they didn't take the field with half a lifetime of dominance behind them, as teams in more recent years have done.

Well into the game, with the scores at 10-4 in favour of Australia, some may have thought that the home side was still in with a shout. Well, the game finished 40-4. The tourists had enough in reserve to put themselves out of sight and Wayne Pearce's try sums up the vast difference between the two teams.

It starts 20 metres from the Australian line with a diagonal run to the right by Max Krilich, the hooker and team captain. He passes inside to Craig Young, the number eight prop forward. When he takes the ball, he's faced with a defensive line. On meeting the tacklers he ducks and shoves, his sheer power enabling him to break through. Now prop forwards are supposed to have power. What spectators did not expect from them in those days was pace.

When Craig Young breaks through the line, he accelerates and leaves the cover behind. Approaching ten metres inside the Great Britain half, Young has support to his left where a teammate is arriving at speed. It was a copybook pass, committing the fullback and giving the supporting player an open field.

But there are still 40 metres to run and the receiving player is a second row forward called Wayne Pearce. In that era you might have expected the cover defence to gain ground on a forward in the clear. But Wayne Pearce not only scores, his pace takes him away from the defence and he goes in under the posts. When more scores followed, it was clear that the 1982 Australians were in a completely different league from Great Britain.

"It was too easy," was a summary voiced at the time. And, as we know, the 1982 tourists went on to win all 22 of their games in Britain and France to enter rugby league history as the *Invincibles*.

As I've said already, a team with superior speed and strength will always win in rugby league. With these areas matched, teamwork and tactics become crucial. With similar capabilities in all these areas, then it's often stealth, individual skill that makes the difference.

The 1982 First Test between Great Britain and the Australian *Invincibles* illustrates this perfectly. By the 1980s, the Australians had already embraced the kind of professionalism that demanded the highest standards of fitness and strength. They worked at both as part of the job. They'd also improved coaching and training at club level, so when players came into the representative side, they could slot into specific roles and everyone had the professionalism to play to order. In the early 1980s, when almost all of the Great Britain players still had only a part-time commitment to the game, the result was nothing less than a mismatch.

Wayne Pearce's try illustrated that difference perfectly. A hooker, a prop forward and a second row had outpaced the Great Britain defence. They had handled the ball like half-backs and shown that teamwork was second nature. And, their move stretched almost 70 metres. It was a try that illustrated clearly the dawn of a new era for rugby league. British teams did get there, but it took another decade, at least.

32 – Henry Paul

The career of Henry Paul is a perfect illustration of how the two codes of rugby have changed in the last decade and a half. And I'm sure there's a book to be written featuring only the subject of deals done to sign him. Just look at the history!

In the early 1990s, as a teenager, Henry played union at school and league at weekends. At the time, in theory at least, that scenario would have been impossible in Britain. But during my playing years I met many professionals who had done exactly this. Any teenager in the rugby league heartlands who went to a school that was still run like a grammar of old would have played rugby union on games afternoons. It was common for such schools to ban rugby league from being played. But of course most people who were any good at the game – at least the most talented amongst them – would also sign up with the local amateur rugby league side or even the junior team of the local professional club. I've no doubt that several youngsters who've represented England at union over the years were in this category, but no doubt rugby union officialdom would probably deny it.

But the two codes in New Zealand have never suffered from this ideological and social class divide. Clearly union has always been the bigger game in the country, but league's following has been secure and I'm sure that New Zealand's victory in the 2008 World Cup will give the local game a real boost.

So, for Henry Paul, growing up playing both rugby codes was nothing special. But when he came to play in England, this put him a huge step ahead of the game, and allowed him to cherry-pick opportunities. Usually the cherry being picked, however, was Henry Paul!

On leaving New Zealand, Henry played a season with Wakefield Trinity. We're pre-Super League here, and he was still a teenager. In 24 games he scored no less than 111 points for the club. It was in that 93-94 season that Henry Paul was responsible for one of the lowest moments in my career, of which he takes great pride in reminding me, I might add. Things weren't going that well for me at the time. I'd started the season late after returning from a stint in Australia with Eastern Suburbs and was nursing a dislocated shoulder. I'd had a shoulder reconstruction which meant I didn't have a proper pre-season. Anyway, to cut a long story short, the Wigan faithful were on my back shouting, "Offiah must go" in response to my lacklustre performances. During our home league fixture with Wakefield that year a bouncy Henry Paul only managed to skip round me on my bad-shoulder side, poke me in the eye, accidentally of course, and score a try. The chorus of hostility I received from the stands that day, from my own supporters, was unparalleled and to make things worse I couldn't see out of the eye for the rest of the game! It was a very low point indeed, especially with Talk of 'Inga the winga' coming. I knew that with Jason Robinson in great form as well, something had to give as three into two doesn't go.

After poking me in the eye, Henry went back to New Zealand only to become a detail in a complicated agreement between two clubs. The arrangement took Andy Platt to Auckland Raiders, who were to compete in the Australian league, and Henry Paul to Wigan Warriors. Apparently, people at Wigan were impressed when he scored a couple of tries against us and poked me in the eye. I think I've heard a story like that before! The quality of his performances at Wakefield had clearly turned heads. After joining in 1994, he stayed with Wigan until 1998, played 187 games and scored 550 points and lost at basketball to me many times. Revenge was so sweet!

His move to Bradford Bulls was described as the worst kept secret in rugby league. His younger brother, Robbie, was already at the club and together they promised to form a formidable half-back partnership. And that is exactly what they did. Henry played just 100 games for Bradford, but scored almost 1000 points. In the meantime, he won 23 caps for New Zealand.

Then, in 2001, another badly kept secret took him to Gloucester to play rugby union in a lucrative deal. But it was not love at first sight. He'd already considered other possibilities in both Australia and New Zealand, but the terms with Gloucester were too good to turn down, despite Bradford's continued claims that he was going to stay with them. Now that's what I call being in demand!

Initially things didn't go well. There were rumours that he would go back to league. But after a switch of position he became a real favourite with the Gloucester fans. He even won six caps for England rugby union – remember he already had 23 caps with New Zealand rugby league – but perhaps even for Henry Paul the union switch was just too late in his career for him to have a real impact in the international arena.

But the story isn't finished. After being voted player of the year by Gloucester fans in 2004 and being nominated for Zurich premiership Player Of The Year, he returned to league with Harlequins. He was already in his early thirties by then and, ironically, in his first game back in Super League he faced brother Robbie who was by then playing for Salford City Reds.

And he's still in demand. Leeds Carnegie and a return to union became the next destination. Henry Paul is now 35. Ten years earlier, I had been a trailblazer in this kind of move when I went to Bedford. But for me the changes were all too late.

Henry Paul won every honour in rugby league, except a World Cup. I'm sure he hoped to achieve much the same in union, but it didn't happen. Had he moved at the same age as Jason Robinson, perhaps, he might have played more international games. We'll never know. And, after all, there was only one season between their moves.

A recurring theme in this sequence of tries is that great tries tend to be scored on great occasions. There are occasional examples of truly outstanding teamwork or individual effort, but usually tries that live in the memory are the ones that win trophies or edge out old foes. Occasionally, when players achieve the very highest standards, their performance becomes iconic, even immortal, despite their finishing on a losing side. I've already described brother Robbie's try at Wembley when the Bulls lost, and here is Henry's, again from a game his team lost. And in both cases, the brothers picked up the man of the match award!

In 1999, a week before the Super League Grand Final, Bradford Bulls had hammered St Helens 40-4 in the qualifying semi-final. But Saints made it through to the final to face the Bulls again. The showdown proved to be a hard, tough, close affair, low-scoring and full of controversy. Henry Paul won the Harry Sunderland Trophy, in just the same way that his brother won the Lance Todd at Wembley. And, again, similar to Robbie, he won it on a losing side, Saints taking the trophy 8-6. The Bulls had a try by Leon Pryce disallowed for a Michael Withers knock-on. It remains a major talking point to this day. What is beyond dispute is the quality of Henry Paul's performance on the night and the outstanding achievement of his first-half try.

In many ways it was similar to Robbie's try at Wembley. Henry's try is apparently more straightforward, more an assertion of pure strength and speed rather than the stealth that characterised his brother's try. But there's a real twist.

There's a scrum, just left of centre. Robbie Paul picks up at the base and feeds Henry at stand-off. A challenge comes in quickly. It's the Saints fullback Paul Atcheson. Where did he come from? Don't know. But we can see where he goes! Henry Paul does a lightning step to his left and bypasses the tackle. But Sonny Nickle is straight on him. There's a hand-off and a shrug and suddenly Henry has a yard of space. Henry is no waster at close to 100 kilos. He's a hard package to grab.

It's 60 metres to the line and Henry explodes into the space where the fullback might have been. But Nickle, a second row forward known for his pace, is just behind in hot pursuit.

There seems to be a fixed gap between them as they sprint. But then Nickle seems to gain. It takes less than ten seconds but it seems to be a whole act from a drama.

Nickle makes his tackle and nails his man. But watch Henry Paul! He's already dipped – not dived, but dipped. He's gained a touch of momentum from our old friend gravity. Don't dive, because you have to work against that force of the earth. Fall, lean into the force that then pulls you, adds to your speed.

On a dry pitch he finishes short. On a greasy surface in October 1999, his momentum makes the score – under the posts. Then, as a flurry of limbs tangle at the end of the action, notice that Henry Paul's feet are different colours – because he's lost a boot! Two feet scampered across the turf, but only one of them had a grip. Amazing!

If you've never sprinted on a greasy, wet grassy pitch in your stocking feet with a world-class sprinting second row forward ready to pounce on your back, I suggest you try it.

33 – Anthony Sullivan

County cups in Lancashire and Yorkshire were contested for the last time in 1993, when Wigan won on one side of the Pennines and Wakefield Trinity on the other. Current fans of the game might not be aware of the status that these knockout competitions occupied throughout their eighty-six year history. Teams went out to win the encounters. These were not competitions offering just window dressing to league commitments. When we look, for instance, at the crowd in attendance at the Lancashire Cup semi-final between St Helens and Wigan in 1991, we can get some feel of the significance of the occasion. Nevertheless, the county cups are firmly things of the past.

When Clive Sullivan became a league professional in the 1960s, he severed ties with union for good. He settled in Hull and, in 1968, was blessed with a son, Anthony, who wanted to follow in his father's footsteps. And he did just that, only the other way round.

Like his father, Anthony Sullivan became one of the game's greatest wingers. He began his career with Hull KR and was soon snapped up by St Helens for whom he played more than 300 games, scoring over 200 tries. When he played for Hull KR, I remember playing against him and thinking he looked a good player, but he seemed to get so much better when he joined St Helens. It might have been because he was in a better team, or possibly because expectations in Hull were so high it put him under pressure. But he just seemed to get better as time went by.

Anthony Sullivan was 22 years old when he turned out for Saints in the 1991 Lancashire Cup semi-final against Wigan. In that game he scored a classic winger's try that was spectacular not for its execution, but for its opportunism. By including this try in my *50 Of The Best*, I can recognise the achievement of a great winger and also make another important point about the game.

I've already mentioned luck. When it runs your way, take your chance. If it goes against you, don't dwell on it. But what about when the opposition loses the plot? In Jamie Lyon's featured try, I recorded 11 attempted tackles, none of which stopped the ball. On balance, however, it was the skill, speed and stealth of the St Helens teamwork that won through. In the Lancashire Cup tie of 1991 the same club, Wigan, is defending against St Helens. This time, they attempt ten tackles in one move. But in that game not only do they not stop the ball, no one apparently gets a hand on a player. So what should St Helens do? The answer is simple. They must take advantage, and they do.

The move starts ten metres inside the Saints half, right-side. Prop forward Neil plays the ball and dummy half Paul Groves feeds infield to George Mann. Now he was a formidable human being, a giant of a second row, built of concrete and always hard to stop.

He actually runs mainly cross-field, but look at the string of Wigan players he draws in. He's on the left when he finally offloads to centre Ropati. He hasn't gained much ground, but he has left the defensive line in tatters.

Ropati advances infield towards halfway. He has plenty of attention from tacklers, all ineffective. A pass to his left finds fullback Tanner who makes a superb run through poor tackling. When the cover actually threatens, he has Anthony Sullivan in support on the left wing and he scores a classic winger's try, heading towards the corner into free space.

Now I'm sure that Anthony Sullivan scored many greater tries than that, and on bigger occasions. But what this try demonstrates is the devastation that a player like George Mann can wreak on a defensive line, even though there's no clean break. He is big, strong, awkward and quick. He can hand-off, turn in a tackle and offload. If you can stop him early you must. But don't go at him one at a time. If he gets space, he'll have your defence all over the place. Then it's up to his teammates to take advantage and, via Anthony Sullivan, Saints did exactly that.

Opportunities can be created in many ways – via a decisive break, a drive or a tactical kick. On this occasion, it's a combination that pulls the defensive line this way and that, leaving it in tatters. But eventually the score is made by brilliant support play and is completed by a winger who knows his job and can deliver exactly what's required by being in the right place at the right time to score.

Sully is just three years younger than me. His career with Saints was outstanding and included three Super League titles, a Challenge Cup and a World Club Challenge. He was capped by Great Britain six times and also played for Wales.

But at the age of 29, he played two seasons of rugby union for Cardiff and was capped by Wales in a second code.

In some ways, Anthony did exactly what his father did, but in reverse, starting in Hull with league and finishing in Cardiff with union. So, in one generation the codes had seen a complete about-face. By 2003, the transformation was complete. In fact when Anthony Sullivan switched and joined Cardiff, Iestyn Harris, another player who'd made his name in league, was already there.

34 – Mike Gregory

Truly great tries are scored on great occasions. So surely there is none greater than Mike Gregory's famous score in July 1988, a try that has since immortalised him in rugby league folklore.

The touring Great Britain Lions had already lost the first two tests, and with them the series, so arriving at the sparsely populated Sydney football stadium, it was obvious we were playing for credibility as well as pride.

Rugby league players are professionals. They take pride in their professionalism. Press reports that the Lions would be easy meat really hurt, though no one would admit it at the time.

So 9 July 1988 was as much of an occasion as any other Great Britain-Australia test match. Australia had won the last four series, whitewashing us each time. They'd chalked up 15 straight wins and Wally Lewis and his Aussies knew they had to emulate past achievements to secure their own glory and, perhaps, more importantly even to save face. They wanted to win, you can be sure of that, so the significance of the occasion matched the greatness of its setting.

But it's this history of Great Britain versus Australia games that gives Mike Gregory's try that day the X-factor, the special something that makes it truly iconic, perhaps immortally so. Not since Odsal Stadium in 1979 had Great Britain beaten the Aussies, and the 1988 team, branded 'the no-hopers' by their hosts, had something to prove.

Despite the fact that most people describe it as a great solo effort, its execution relied much on both tactics and teamwork. I need to justify that, because if all you see is a 75-metre run by a try-scorer, it looks like a purely individual effort. But it's what led up to the score that interests me.

The game was in the balance. We were ahead, but at Australia 12 - Great Britain 20, a score against us would have really threatened. There was plenty of time left. Things had turned against us late in the game on so many previous occasions that, if it happened again in Sydney, no one would even have commented.

Australia played the ball on the last tackle of their set. They were on our left, their right, about 30 metres out. Wally Lewis received and fed Jackson. The Aussie commentator's voice rose because there was a half-break. It's amazing how much can happen in a split second in our game, because, when Jackson fed O'Connor further left, there was real anticipation of a scoring chance. But O'Connor spilled it and the ball ran loose, hacked on. Henderson Gill picked it up.

Now he could have just stuffed it up his jersey and run forward into the tacklers. It would have been safe and straightforward. But he didn't do that. At half-time Malcolm Reilly had impressed on us how important it was to stay positive, to go out and win the game rather than avoid losing it.

So Henderson Gill sets off cross-field. He picks up near the right touchline and is tackled midfield, under our posts, still only five metres from the line. But his run has gained us vital split seconds, long enough for our side to get back behind the ball and regroup. He's also moved the play away from the wing, and the Aussies haven't regrouped. I step up to dummy half, as this was the part of the game I loved. I'd always sniff about dummy half, looking to get my hands on the ball, but David Hulme pushes me aside. He knows the best play is a simple consolidating forward push. He takes the ball and runs forward to gain a few more metres. We're all in position by then.

When he plays the ball, Andy Gregory runs from dummy half. He goes right at a slight angle, but at full pelt. He slips through two tacklers. It looks like they get in each other's way, but funnily enough it's Andy's pace that forces an error.

It's then that teamwork really comes into play because a half-break isn't enough. Mike Gregory has seen the chance and follows. His backing-up gives Andy the chance to slip the ball, just a short pass to his left, before the hit comes in from Ettinghausen. And so Mike Gregory is in the clear, but it's still 75 metres to the line. I'm just behind and to Mike's left. "This is my try," are the words going through my mind. I know I can outpace anyone. So I accelerate, sprinting to Mike's left.

It's then that Wally Lewis pulls my shirt as I go past him. Wally wasn't the fastest player, but he was very shrewd and never missed a trick. Mike Gregory, God rest his soul, knows all along he can make the line, and he does. All that is left for me is to follow on behind and celebrate. The try and conversion make the score 12-26. You're never comfortable against the Aussies, but that was three scores ahead and it felt great. "The Union Jack has waited a long time to fly high in rugby league circles internationally, but boy, oh boy, it's flying high this afternoon," the Australian match commentator said.

I rang Mike Gregory just before he died in 2007 from muscular atrophy, a form of motor neurone disease. I spoke to him about that try, a score that has surely immortalised him in the history of our game. It was a great individual effort, but positive tactics and superb teamwork set it up. All the more fitting then that such an important try should have been scored by the player that Ellery Hanley later described as 'a great British soldier' and Sean Edwards called 'a warrior, full of life, full of fun'.

35 – I get noticed

In my first two seasons at Widnes we won both the First Division Championship and the Premiership. In 1988 we beat St Helens in the last league match of the season and similarly in 1989 Wigan to secure the Championship. In both games I managed to score hat-tricks!

In 1988 we beat St Helens again in the Premiership final and in 1989 Hull. So in my first two seasons in rugby league I had two Championships, two Premierships and a World Club Challenge to my name. These were significant honours, major landmarks in my career. There have been great players in this great game who have never got their names on any major honour. And here was I, a lad from London, who held five major honours in the game within two seasons of starting out. There's no wonder I remember vividly some of the tries from those landmark games.

But one of the tries that secured those league leadership honours really stands out. It's a try that could make it into any selection of great tries. But for me it was special for another, very important reason. The try was the third of my hat-trick against Wigan in 1989. It was a try born out of teamwork. But I finished it with an input of real individualism and it was an input that was noticed.

The move starts at a play-the-ball just over 20 metres from our line, just right of the posts. Acting half-back Phil McKenzie dummies right and then swivels right round to set off left. He drives forward and releases to his left. The receiver Richie Eyres passes quickly to the left again to Widnes prop, Joe Grimmer. He has two Wigan tacklers approaching, Ellery Hanley and a second row who I think was Andy Platt, but I could be wrong. They are just about to make the tackle when Joe does something quite bright.

His next supporting player to the left is tightly marked. The Wigan tackler is clearly going to make the tackle just as the receiver gets the ball. So the Widnes prop has the vision to spot me unmarked out wide and hoists a lobbed pass over the top. The ball comes to me. I'm ten metres inside my own half. I have Tony Iro in front. He's stayed wider than me, effectively closing down the space on the left wing, forcing me towards the cover defence. So, uncharacteristically for me, I set off inside. I cross halfway, and the Wigan cover is coming across. I have to step further inside to my right to wrong-foot a Wigan player.

Then there's a gap ahead, ironically between the two Wigan wingers, Tony Iro and Mark Preston. I go for it and get through. But now fullback Steve Hampson is straight ahead.

I was at the end of my second season at Widnes. I already knew everything I needed to know about Naughton Park. I was especially familiar with the hill up that left touchline, because I'd spent a good proportion of my time running up and down it! I might add as a footnote here the importance of knowing where you are on a pitch. Many of the tries in my *50 Of The Best* are scored without the benefit of home advantage. But as I've said, the reason for including this home try of my own was its larger significance, not its local glory.

There's space on the left wing, of course, because my marker on that side has come inside to cover. By then he's behind me. I've just gone past him! If you're confident of your pace then running a bit further is actually to your advantage. I know I can do them all for speed.

So I set off towards the touchline, the winger's friend. I have to use every inch of width to round the fullback, but that's exactly what I do. When I get to the corner I'm still on a slight diagonal and almost finish up over the touchline in goal. But I ground the ball. Both Wigan wingers are just behind me, by then spectating.

The first player to come and congratulate me almost had to save me from the crowd, along with referee John Holdsworth. I was being mobbed by fans and everyone was jubilant, to say the least. The player that rescued me and patted me on the back was our loose forward, Richie Ayers, the same Richie Ayers that would be sent off at Wembley four years later for a high tackle on yours truly! By then, of course, I was a Wigan player and we played the 1993 final against Widnes, my old club.

Now I've already mentioned that it's often the context, the setting and the occasion that make a particular try truly memorable. Well, for me and my career that try was enormously significant. It secured another trophy for my team and another honour for myself. It was another record to add to a growing list. But it was for none of these reasons that, for me, this try was significant.

It was on seeing that try that Maurice Lindsay said that he wanted me at Wigan. It didn't happen immediately, but it did happen – and the rest is history. And it was that try, at least in my mind, that made it all possible. I have to include it in my *50 Of The Best*!

36 & 37 – Kevin Penny

There've been players such as Shaun Edwards and Danny McGuire who were born in the rugby league heartlands and clearly raised with the game in their blood. I've mentioned players who were brought up on rugby union, such as Brian Carney, Clive Sullivan and myself, and moved to rugby league to pursue careers as professional sportsmen.

But how about a player who was apparently destined for honours in a completely different sport and then took up rugby league? There've been over the years a number of sprinters who became professional rugby league players. Berwyn Jones did it successfully in the 1960s. Dwain Chambers attempted it recently with the opposite result.

But, how about a basketball player? And how about a player who had not even played rugby league until the age of 16, breaking into Super League as a 19-year-old and setting the game alight? Well that happened in 2007 in the shape of Kevin Penny.

You will already have gathered from my *50 Of The Best* that I have a soft spot for wingers and a keen eye for features of wing play. That's why I was so excited a couple of years ago when Kevin made his mark on the game. I'm on record as having said that he could do things that I used to do, things that I'd rarely seen from wingers since I retired from the game. Kevin even managed a fly-hack try against Salford in his first season, which is a real rarity in the game these days.

I want to feature two of Kevin Penny's tries. Both are scored for Warrington against St Helens. Both are scored in Challenge Cup ties, one in 2007 and one the next year. Ironically, Warrington lost both games!
Together they illustrate different aspects of the winger's game. In the first, Kevin Penny is presented with an overlap and a touchline to hug. In the second, he runs from deep and has to make the try with much more than pure speed.

In 2007, Kevin Penny was a rookie. He'd played only a handful of senior games when Warrington came up against Saints in the Challenge Cup quarter final at Knowlsley Road. His try that day was a copybook piece of wing play.

From a play-the-ball five metres inside the Saints' half, centre-field, the ball goes left. Sullivan, Briers, Grose and Clarke handle, and there are a couple of miss-passes and dummy runs. As often happens when the ball moves quickly to the wing with dummy runs along the way, the opposition winger gets drawn in and there's an overlap. So when Kevin Penny receives on the left wing he has space. But he is still more than 40 metres from the line.

Now, you can tell real pace. It leaves defenders literally flailing in its wake. As Kevin Penny steams down the left touch line, three Saints defenders get across. But in turn, each one is half a metre short and their lunges connect only with fresh air. Gidley, Gardner and Wellens are each at full stretch, but for all of them Kevin Penny's pace is a stretch too far. He goes in at the corner. It was a classic winger's score, but a score that few wingers would have completed. Not much gets past Paul Wellens, but this flying rookie did!

In May the following year, the two teams met again in a Challenge Cup tie on the same ground. The game was again hard-fought, but this time there was only one score between the sides at the end. St Helens again won, but the lead see-sawed back and forth in a pulsating game. In the first half Kevin Penny scored what has been described as a dream try. It's one of those rare occasions, like a try I scored at Hull in 1994, where the move actually goes more than the length of the field.

Saints have just put up a high ball that's dropping just in the field of play, right under the Warrington crossbar. If you take the ball and go to ground, the chances are you'll be bundled over your own goal line by the tacklers. Do anything else and you take a risk. It could easily lead to a lost ball, a dropped pass or an opposition score, or all three!

But the Warrington defender takes his chance and immediately flicks the ball back to Hicks who receives a good two metres behind his own line.

Now he has only one route and that's into the field of play. Defenders and attackers alike have been drawn in to centre-field so he sets off towards the space on the Warrington left. He does a brilliant job along a diagonal, taking play 15 metres from his goal line. Then, when the tacklers are about to bring him down, he slips a beautiful pass out to his left to find Kevin Penny who is still well within his own 20-metre line.

He has space ahead. His blistering speed takes him to almost halfway before Sean Long appears as a cover defender tracking cross-field from behind the play – he'd just kicked the ball! Kevin Penny takes a step infield to wrong-foot and beat the tackler. He straightens immediately, but the step off his left foot has given the cover a split second to gain on him and Fa'asavalu is within range.

Kevin Penny's response, and done without even breaking his stride, is to apply a classic hand-off, the 'big don't argue', with his right arm. This puts him in the clear. Now it's a straight race to the line and here's where you can really see Kevin Penny's pace. The defenders are simply not going to get near.

When he touches down at the corner, the move has covered 103 metres and Kevin Penny has carried the ball for over 80 of them, has outpaced defenders, used a hand-off and beaten a tackle with a sidestep. What more could you ask for?

Well, in Kevin Penny's case, the extra that the coach wanted was a better all-round performance in other aspects of the game, particularly in defence. This was highlighted in the second half of the same game when he spilled a ball near to his own corner flag and gifted a try to Saints. And remember that there was only one score between the teams at the end.

In 2009, Kevin Penny's star didn't shine as I and some others had predicted. He spent the season on loan to Widnes Vikings, presumably to give him a chance to demonstrate to the powers that be in Warrington that he had confronted and strengthened those weaknesses. His two tries for Widnes in their Northern Rail Cup Final triumph over Barrow at Bloomfield Road, Blackpool, will have done much to restore his confidence and profile.

What remains undeniable is Kevin Penny's pace and attacking flair along the wing. What also seems to be true is that in the modern game a player like Kevin Penny could be considered a luxury that Warrington can't afford. Or some might just say he needs to present a more rounded game. Everything else aside, he's definitely the kind of player that excites crowds.

38 – Danny McGuire

Danny McGuire surely has rugby league running in his veins. In a complex, international world of television rights, contracts and pragmatism, shifts from league to union and back again, Danny McGuire seems to be a young player plucked from a different era, the time when local lads made good. You can almost feel the pride he still feels turning out in that Leeds shirt that as a boy he dreamt of wearing.

And what a contrast with another Leeds lad, Gary Schofield. There's no more or less talent, no more or less precociousness, no more or less ability, speed, strength or tactical awareness, but what a gulf there already exists in terms of achievement! Danny McGuire's career, despite the fact he's only in his mid-twenties, has already ensured his legacy in the game's role of honours.

Every weekend, on hundreds of pitches across the country, potentially great players score undoubtedly great tries. But that's as far as they go. It's only when the setting and the stage builds them up that they become iconic, truly memorable. Where Gary Schofield's career didn't take him, Danny McGuire's has already visited. It reminds us all that no matter how talented we think we are, life, like rugby league, is a team game played in our own time. We do not choose our lives. Our actions make our lives, but only after fortune has taken her bite. For some, what remains is less than what was requested. On others, fortune only ever seems to smile. Let's go straight to the try.

Fortune had already smiled on Danny McGuire. After a wait of 32 years, Leeds finally secured a fourth Championship win in the 2004 Grand Final. Danny McGuire scored a try that night in the 16-8 victory over Bradford Bulls. It brought his season's tally to 39. He was 22 years old.

So lady luck had already played a hand in Danny's career. But four years later in 2008, she was to make him a star, not only a try-scorer, but a match-winner. It was a try that embodied all five of the aspects of the game I've used as a thread through my selection.

Danny used strength to shrug off a challenge. He showed remarkable speed to go the long way to the line. Without teamwork the position could not have been created. Overall, tactics won Leeds the game on the night, their style of play calculated to offer them their best chance of winning in the conditions. And stealth? Well, here is what happened. But with all five of the game's elements on his side, he still needed the hand of lady luck to make his name.

The match is in the final quarter. It's 18-16 to Leeds. Saints have just scored. Watch out!

Leeds have a play-the-ball about 20 metres from the Saints line, left of centre. Rob Burrow, Danny McGuire's scrum-half partner, is acting half-back. Two passes go right. Kevin Sinfield receives. Now Kevin is one of the game's thinkers. He won the Harry Sunderland Trophy in the 2004 Grand Final and has developed into one of the game's master tacticians. He's also quite brilliant with the boot.

The October night is wet and greasy. Aren't they all? Two weeks before, Saints had wiped the floor with Leeds 30-0 in the play-offs. But it seems that only one team learned from the experience.

Up goes the kick from Kevin Sinfield. It's on the diagonal to the Leeds right into the corner. It's so perfectly judged, flighted and executed that Francis Meli, the St Helens left wing, who is in perfect position to defend near his corner flag, does not need to move. It's down his throat. But in those circumstances, all he can do is wait. The Leeds rush, however, is approaching at full pelt.

So when the ball arrives, the Leeds players also arrive with their forward momentum and energy. Up they go.

The melee produces a dropped ball. You can't blame the man condemned by the quality of the kick to stand and wait for not getting up. If the kick is that good, the stationary defender is on a loser.
Then lady luck lends her hand. The ball can go anywhere. It can go forward, back, be knocked on, ricochet into touch. The ball does go anywhere. It goes straight to Danny McGuire who gratefully accepts.

Teamwork has created the position. Tactics and stealth delivered the kick. Luck played a hand. Now strength and speed combine to twist Danny McGuire out of the immediate tackle. He spins right round to his left. The tackler comes loose, cast off. Then stealth tells him to head cross-field and speed makes things happen. Speaking of stealth, does he run straight at the referee? Watch the try several times and see what you think…

It was reminiscent of the Ellery Hanley try of 1988, only the other way round, as if reflected in the halfway line. The difference in October 2004 is that Danny McGuire runs 20 metres through a crowd. It's a crowd indeed, with the referee in there somewhere, and no one even lays a finger on him.

Twice Danny McGuire has made decisive scores for Leeds in Grand Finals. This second one won the game. Its place in fans' memories and even the history of the game are assured.

Danny McGuire is the epitome of commitment, ability, ambition and self-belief combined. He's also a Leeds man. It's hard to imagine him playing for anyone else, except, of course, the international side. By the time the World Cup starts in 2013, however, Danny McGuire will be over 30 years old. And that may be a year too far for him. If a home nation is to win the tournament, it may be that a player from a younger generation has to emerge to make an impact. Such a player might just be someone like a young half-back, who has recently graduated from the St Helens academy, a player who will feature a little later in my *50 Of The Best*.

39 – One that might have got away

'Going the length of the field' is one of those iconic rugby league phrases. It's used quite often and, usually, it's not quite accurate. Anything that involves a break followed by a sprint and chase from 20 metres or so from your own line tends to qualify as 'going the length of the field'. Even my 1994 Wembley epic, the best try I've ever scored, was not quite the length of the field. I was about eight metres from our line when I took Franco Botica's pass. So in straight line terms, I carried the ball about 92 metres, not a hundred.

If you think about it, going the length of the field is not at all easy. If you run literally from try-line to try-line you cover a hundred metres. But if you receive the ball on your own try-line, you're probably handicapped by a near-standing start and a frame of mind that has defence as the highest priority. Usually, the last thing on your mind is whether you might run to the other end of the field and score! Most players would opt for a short drive to gain a few metres of safety for your side. And don't forget that if you're pinned right back, the side on the attack is rampant. Their tacklers are going to do the utmost to pin you back.

On 28 October 1994, I played for Wigan in a First Division match against Hull at the Boulevard. It was a hard-fought affair. We ran out winners, but not comfortably. The score was 19-12 and I got two tries on the night. For the first I did genuinely go the length of the field.

Hull were on the attack, just ten metres out on our right flank. They played the ball infield and, just as the Sky Sports commentators said they would surely kick, the Hull prop McNamara did just that. What followed was a piece of pure luck. That kick could have grubbered through towards the posts and been touched down by a Hull player. But it hit Barrie McDermott, our prop. In fact, it was hand-to-ball, not ball-to-hand. It ricocheted into the air and ballooned up towards our line. Though wrong-footed, our fullback Paul Atcheson caught the ball to his left just before it bounced. His left forearm was actually over the try-line, but he'd deliberately grounded the ball with his right arm just a coat of paint infield. Play on.

He stands up and plays the ball. The passes go to our left, towards my wing. When Henry Paul feeds the ball to me at the end of the line, I'm barely ten metres to the left of the posts. I have three Hull players in attendance and I'm just about one metre from our line. Thanks, Henry!

I did what worked for me so often. If you can find space, you can run. And there's space wide to the left. But I have a marker. My opposite number, Hull right wing Danby, is ready to tackle and beyond him is his centre Tevita Vaikona, who's already dropped back to cover. I stall, threatening to shift inside, but I'm always going to head for the space on the flank!

I accelerate past Danby. Vaikona comes across and gets both hands on me. I don't hand him off. It's more of a shrug, but I'm moving fast by then. I'm not even up to halfway when fullback Gary Nolan comes across. I do the swerve in and out routine, but there's space on the left touchline so I head for it. By the time I cross the Hull ten-metre line, I'm round him and completely clear. Basically, the Hull tacklers have tackled one another!

Stand-off Shane Endacott makes a valiant effort to get back. He's never going to catch me, but he does keep me out wide. That's another example of professionalism. It would have been easy for him to have just given up. But he didn't and, as a result, I couldn't risk heading further infield.

So by the time I touch down, I've gone 99 metres with the ball. My run had actually started from within our own in-goal area. Now that's what I call a 'going the length of the field'!

I've said that to achieve the status of a great score, a try needs an occasion and a stage. So how is it that a try from a league game 15 years ago manages to make it into my selection? Well, there are two parts to the answer. First, this is my choice of *50 Of The Best* and this try represents one of the few occasions in my career that I did go literally the length of the field. Second, the reason it exists at all was that one of the guys on Sky TV remembered the score and unearthed the video for me, otherwise it would remain forgotten. When we read through the tries I've included here it's worth thinking how much of the game and how many achievements of its players have drifted into obscurity. Let's have other versions of *50 Of The Best* to reinstate some of them!

40 & 41 – Mark Calderwood

The one thing you know for certain in rugby league is that nothing is for certain! Don't count your chickens in this game. Tomorrow is always another day. So how about this 'Roy of the Rovers' story?

Your debut is 2001. Your first try is in a Challenge Cup semi-final against St Helens. It wins the Eddie Waring Memorial as the best try in the competition. In the two full seasons that follow, you are your club's top try scorer. And in the next season you pick up a Grand Final winners' medal. A year later you're Super League's top try scorer. By now you've scored 106 ties in 143 appearances for your club.

And then you decide that a change is as good as a rest. You don't renew your contract and then take a two-year deal with a big name club in search of some even greater honours. Does this sound familiar? Is this another Martin Offiah try?

When I left Widnes in January 1992, I'd won everything on offer in rugby league at the time except the Challenge Cup at Wembley. It's ironic, because Widnes used to be called 'the Cup Kings'!

When we played Wigan – especially on the big occasions – we generally did well. Our record was good. But in the early 1990s, it was clear that I needed a change, a new challenge that could make an already successful career into a great one. My tries against Wigan had caught the eye. For me the change worked.

I joined the most successful club ever in rugby league. We won a hatful of honours. Wigan topped the league for eight straight years and I was part of that. Perhaps ironically, perhaps not, the last season in the club's run was 1995-6. Now guess the year that I left Wigan!

So what about our successful try scorer who decided to move? Well, of course, it's Mark Calderwood. For me, a move worked. It made my career. For Mark, well, it didn't.

Mark could have been a great winger, rather than a very

good one. In 2006, when his Wigan career began, assessments of his future might have assumed continued success and greater achievement. Mark's own words after the 2005 Grand Final loss with Leeds reveal what he thought lay ahead. "I am going to a good team and I am sure I can be successful with them." Newspaper articles spoke of him as the new Billy Boston or Martin Offiah. Comparisons are never useful, however. What they should have said is that if he's lucky he's going to be the new Mark Calderwood.

Now I've mentioned luck a few times. It plays a significant part in any game and rugby league is no exception. Luck, after all, plays a part in life! When I changed clubs, it worked. I scored tries. I fitted in. Wigan's 2006 season, however, was a poor one. They struggled. Relegation threatened. They lost more games than they won and the final points difference was negative. Mark Calderwood took three months to score his first try. And then luck played her hand when he sustained an injury that sidelined him. He scored only a handful of tries that season.

The following year was an improvement. He developed a good understanding with fullback Chris Ashton. There was a length-of-the-field try against his old club at Headingley when the two of them combined after Mark picked up a loose ball. This loose ball is becoming something of a theme!

There was also an amazing hat-trick at the end of the 2007 season. Perhaps this was the high point of Mark's time at Wigan. It certainly made headlines and a couple of years later the game is still remembered as one of the great comebacks in Super League history.

The Wigan side of 2006 was clearly not a happy bunch. In 2007, things had obviously improved because they finished fifth to earn a play-off place. The first game was against Bradford Bulls at Odsal and the home side was rampant for almost three quarters of the game. They were leading 30-6 after 55 minutes and most people in the ground probably thought the game was over. Question marks about Mark's defensive play were as big as ever, since an error of his might just have contributed to the Bradford tally. But we won't dwell on that. If you score a hat-trick to win a game, who cares about the own goal?

In the game's next 20 minutes, Wigan scored 31 points to win the match. A drop goal on 76 minutes by Pat Richards broke the tie. But in the meantime, Mark Calderwood scored three tries, the third of which was the quintessence of speed.

The second was a classic winger's try. The ball moved right to the touchline against a stretched defence. The score was made by a long pass from Trent Barratt, the talented Australian. It still needed scoring, but the pass was a peach and in itself created the opportunity. It's interesting to reflect that this superb player completed only half of his contract with Wigan, ostensibly because of his wife's homesickness. He left at the same time Mark Calderwood went to Hull. And the two of them were not alone in leaving.

Mark Calderwood's third try in that game came with the score on 30-24. Bradford were attacking, trying to stop the rot. A score would have killed the game, a game that a few minutes before they thought they'd already slaughtered.

Bradford are driving towards the Wigan 20-metre line, near centre-field. The ball is played and goes left. Shontayne Hape, now close to the Bradford left, attempts an offload in the tackle. David Solomona, who was unstoppable in the earlier part of the game, threatened to power over the Wigan line for a decisive try. But the ball went to ground.

For all the world it looks like a pair of Bradford hands have grabbed it. But then an express train comes through. Almost before the action can be seen, Mark Calderwood has gathered about 17 metres from his own line.

OK, he had a head start. OK, it's an interception try. OK, the game's in the last quarter and everyone's tired – including Mark Calderwood! But it's 83 metres – more on the angle – to the posts at the other end.

But does he accelerate! And when he goes in under the posts, he's still accelerating away from his pursuers. The speed is simply awesome. And then, of course, Wigan go on to win the game.

What this, perhaps the greatest comeback in Super League history, demonstrates is that you can never take anything for granted in rugby league. Luck plays a part, but players can make things happen. These days, Mark Calderwood needs a comeback of his own. Surely he has the ability.

When I arrived at Widnes, I was taken under the substantial wing of Dougie Laughton. When Dougie was at Widnes, he was one of the most successful coaches in the game. But his philosophy was quite low-key. He matched on-the-pitch expectations with the strengths his players offered. Management thus became a process of identifying what players were naturally good at and then sending them out to deliver what they knew.

When the Wigan players were 30-6 down, what did they have to lose? The game was already lost, so, if you have any pride left, have a go at what you do best. Mark Calderwood scored three classic winger's tries in that frame of mind. And look at the result.

Whatever contributed to Mark Calderwood's lack of form at Wigan, only he knows. Let me rephrase that. No one knows. But Mark had all the talent to make him one of the game's greats. At 27 he still has time to make up for some of the lost time, but never bet on the bounce of that ball. A change of clubs worked for me, but for Mark Calderwood it turned sour. Add to that the 'privilege' of playing for England in an abortive World Cup campaign, and you might begin to wonder if lady luck has had your number from the start. Good luck for the future, Mark, and let's see some of that blistering pace that we all know you have.

42 – Gareth Raynor

Sometimes luck can put you in the right place at the right time. Then, if you have the speed, the strength, the tactics and a dose of stealth, you'll probably profit.

By November 2006, Great Britain had not beaten Australia in Australia since 1988 in Sydney. How do 18 years pass by like that? In the meantime, scores of great players will have seen entire careers begin and end. The Great Britain players who took the field on that wet night again in Sydney were in the right place at the right time.

Now there's been much talk of Australia fielding an under-strength team, and that coach Ricky Stuart wanted to experiment with new faces. Try telling that to the players involved – on either side!

The game was part of a tri-nations tournament with New Zealand. Again Australia came through to win the competition, beating New Zealand 16-12 in the final after some lacklustre Great Britain performances against New Zealand and Australia. The tournament seemed more than a little farcical at one stage after New Zealand were docked points for fielding an ineligible player. It seems that having a grandmother can qualify you for national status, whereas having a great-grandmother does not, if you see what I mean! Such is sport.

The Australian press criticised their team for handling errors, defensive weakness and not taking chances. You would think that just once in a while someone might admit they were facing a better side!

For Gareth Raynor, that match was a tail of two tries, one

he did score, and one he didn't, but crucially neither did Australian Ben Hornby.

The game had see-sawed up to the last quarter. Australia took the lead with an interception try. Great Britain levelled when Paul Wellens scored and then went in front when Jamie Peacock powered over in the second half. But Australia levelled again at 12-12. Lee Gilmour was sent through a gap by a Leon Pryce pass to restore the Great Britain lead. With the scores at 12-18 against Australia, there was a pivotal moment.

After 56 minutes, Ben Hornby looked sure to score for Australia in the corner. With scores at 16-18 or 18-18 from the conversion, who knows what the Australians might have done in the last quarter? If they'd gone on to win in those last 20 minutes it would hardly have been a surprise, would it? But, with Hornby en route to the line, winger Gareth Raynor put in a tackle. Not only did he nail his man, he also managed to dislodge the ball and so saved what looked to be a certain try. Tries win matches. Conceding tries loses them. Gareth Raynor's night then went from good to better.

Great Britain then scored a try that, like the Phil Ford try in 1988, also had its lucky bounce. It was a score created by complete stealth, but finished by pure teamwork of the very highest standard.

Australia were in the Great Britain half, wide to their left, hard up against the touch line. From the play-the-ball, they made two passes infield to the right. Then, there's an error. A poor offload goes to ground. In 1988, when

Great Britain did something similar, the ball bounced up gently into Andy Gregory's hands and Phil Ford scored the try. In November 2005, it was a boot that made contact: Sean Long's boot.

The ball goes high in a lob. Sean Long pursues. It has to bounce. It's travelled too far to allow a clean take. And so it bounces – bounces beautifully up, so Sean Long can take it knee-height, even in stride. But he's not quite clear.

He runs over halfway, but the cover defence is closing in. So what does he do? That's right. He stops! Stops and waits for support! Now that's confidence in your teammates!

And there is St Helens teammate James Roby inside on his left. Long makes the pass and Roby gets to within the 20-metre line before the cover brings him down.

Now a quick break downfield, followed by a chase draws cover across to one side of the field and almost certainly means there is space on the other wing. What's needed is clear. Play the ball quickly, move it along the line as fast as possible and find the space. Sounds simple, doesn't it? But the line has to be in place. Players have to be in position, in spite of the fact that play has seen an unexpected change of possession, followed by a quick, chancy break 50 metres upfield. What's more, they have to handle a wet and greasy ball perfectly and they must work together.

And on this occasion it all comes together. Quick passes

via Paul Wellens and Kirk Yeaman find Gareth Raynor on the left touchline and he goes in at the corner. Copybook stuff!

That score made it 12-22 putting Great Britain two scores clear. There were 76 minutes played, almost 20 minutes after Gareth Raynor's try-saving tackle. I bet those 20 minutes would have been a different story if that tackle hadn't saved a try... Sean Long then dropped a late goal to make the final score 12-23 and confirm a famous Great Britain victory.

And Gareth Raynor? He's on the wing for Hull. He's 31 now, has seven caps and four tries for Great Britain and England. He scored 96 tries from 176 games, all for Hull after just three for Leeds at the start of his career.
His career has never really hit the high spots and, it has to be said, he's had more than his fair share of controversy. But he's been a loyal servant for Hull and an ever-present, despite suffering several injuries.

He played in Sydney only after Danny McGuire's injury forced Leon Pryce to stand-off. But when you have some luck, the trick is to take advantage and both Gareth Raynor and Great Britain did just that.

Oh, by the way, Gareth started in union, went to league, returned to union and then back to league. That's something else that's becoming a bit of a theme!

43 – 500
At the end of my autobiography, the last game I describe

is London Broncos against Bradford Bulls on 31 August 1997. We won the game 28-24 and I scored two tries. It was a pretty momentous time for me. I'd severed my professional links with Wigan the year before to pursue a dual commitment to rugby union with Bedford and league with the Broncos.

In the previous year, my life had turned upside down. I'd left my place in Manchester to move back to London. I'd reinstated my contact with rugby union after a ten-year separation. And I had left Wigan, the most successful club of the era, as well as completing ten years in the game. I'd even been on holiday for the first time to Ibiza where a Spanish waiter asked for my autograph, recognising me by virtue of the hotel piping Sky Sports to all the rooms!

But it was none of these changes that really made the date memorable. It was events outside the sport, outside of my own life that were truly memorable at the end of August 1997.

Occasionally something truly memorable happens, an event that reminds you to keep things in perspective, to keep your feet on the ground and to re-think your priorities. But the day the Broncos beat Bradford Bulls 28-24 didn't stick in my mind because of my two tries. It was because the game was played on the day Diana, Princess of Wales was killed in a Paris car crash.

Now I would bet that most British people can still remember what they were doing that day when they heard the news. A generation earlier – long before my time – President Kennedy was shot dead in Dallas,

Texas. Just about everyone who was around at the time can remember exactly what they were doing that day. It's as if your own everyday activities take on a completely changed status because of their association with a truly momentous, major world event. In this way something quite mundane, completely ordinary can become elevated in importance so that it lives in the memory.

It's the same with events in our personal lives. The greatest things in my life to date have been the birth of my son, Tyler, followed by the birth of my soon to be second child, as yet unnamed. But the third most important event could be a tie – the honours being shared by a certain spectacular Wembley try in 1994 and another, a less spectacular effort and scored on a humbler stage, at the end of June 2001.

Now that second try of the game would certainly not make it into anyone else's selection of great tries. The score itself was a pretty ordinary event. But that try made history in modern rugby league. It was something I'd worked hard for over the years, a milestone that I'd set in the future of my career, a place I'd resolved I would reach. When I got there, ironically, the achievement was made doubly sweet because it also allowed me to make something of a point.

I had four years with the Broncos, but after our defeat by Leeds at Wembley in May 1999, things turned a bit sour. Basically, they let me go. I have no regrets, however, because I'm the type of person who looks ahead to the next challenge rather than dwelling on what might have been in the past. I'd been in the game for 13 seasons by the time I joined Salford City Reds. They weren't at the top of the league, of course. Far from it. They were a side struggling to stay in Super League. I'd had an offer to play union again, but I was within reach of that milestone I'd set myself and, though it was still in the future, it had appeared from over the horizon and I felt it was within my grasp.

I'd scored 458 tries by then and was approaching 34 years of age. I was already the third greatest try-scorer in the game's history, behind Brian Bevan (796) and Billy Boston (571). For most people, I think, there would be little left to achieve. But for me, just being in that list was not good enough. I was clearly not going to challenge Billy Boston's tally, let alone the astronomical heights achieved by Brian Bevan. But the milestone of 500 tries was there. It was within reach and I wouldn't be satisfied until I'd reached it.

Now, I'd lost some motivation around the end of my time with the London Broncos where I'd been for four years. I'd suffered a severe body blow when coach Dan Stains dropped me from the side. That hurt more than a bit.

But the number 500 was fixed in my mind and, for it to count, I had to achieve it while still playing in the game's top flight. We can all be big fish when we live in little ponds, but small fry was not for me.

I kept working hard and gave as much as I had throughout my career. When you get to 34, however, things just don't come as easily. The training gets harder, the knocks last longer and injuries become progressively harder to shrug off. But I kept at it and, sure enough, the number 500 kept coming closer. If you keep going, the line comes to you!

It's ironic that the day I ran out onto the field with 498 tries behind me to start another game of rugby league, it was against London Broncos. I was in my second season with Salford and another year older. That afternoon, not only did I have history within my grasp, I could also make a point. I could make a score and settle a score at the same time.

It was my second score of the game. The try itself wasn't spectacular, just a run in and touch down from close range on my favoured left side. But I knew that I'd achieved something that would probably never again be done in the modern game. And, to add a bit of spice, I'd scored it against the side that had let me go. Brilliant!

I will never forget that try because it made history. No other player in the modern game had reached that milestone and none in the future ever will. Not only was I now the third highest try-scorer of all time, I was over that 500 figure, close enough to Billy Boston to warrant respect. It was hard work indeed to reach that figure, especially when all of them had to be scored against the highest quality opposition. I don't intend to belittle Billy Boston's or Brian Bevan's achievements, but it has to be said that in their eras the county league system did mean that big sides occasionally turned out against minnows.

I must be the last winger to span the modern and older versions of the game. Back in the 1980s, there were still quite a lot of near-amateurs in the game. Most players, even in the top-flight teams, were only semi-professional. And if you'd told me when I left Rosslyn Park to go to Widnes in 1987 that before the end of my career rugby union would have had its own professional league, I would just not have believed you!

This greater professionalism is a wholly good thing, for both codes. It's led to greater dedication amongst the players, higher standards of fitness and strength, greater athleticism and more highly developed technique. It's also made both games tougher defensively. This means that most teams can no longer afford to field what I call throw-back wingers, players like myself who were dedicated to converting opportunities into scores.

In addition, given the greater pace and strength in the game, given also the greater training requirements and the necessity for all players to practise and then perfect their defensive skills before anything else, I think it will be hard for any player to last 15 seasons at the top of the game with the demands that rugby league makes on a player's body.

When I scored try number 501 for Salford against Wakefield, I'd already attended a ceremony at the Lowry Arts Centre to mark the 500. I knew that my playing days were over. There was nothing left to achieve. I'd reached my dream, a mark that will remain, never to be forgotten or denied, and probably never to be matched.

44 & 45 – Leon Pryce

I have two tries from Leon Pryce. Ironically, one is for

Bradford against St Helens in a match Bradford lost, while the other is for St Helens, helping them achieve Grand Final success against Hull. The tries illustrate two important aspects of the game today.

Leon Pryce came from a rugby league family. Bradford born, at 16 he was captain of England schools. Bradford Bulls was his obvious professional home and he signed for them while still a teenager.

Success came quickly. He appeared in five Grand Finals for the club, winning three and collecting the Harry Sunderland Trophy in 2005. He was capped for England while still a teenager. But the thing that he really wanted to do was play at stand-off and that opportunity at Bradford didn't exist.

In 2006 he became a St Helens player and has gone on to achieve more success with them in a Grand Final and also in the Challenge Cup. He also has the Lance Todd Trophy to his name.

But Leon's career has not been without its blemishes. His disciplinary record, both on and off the field, has done him no favours. In the context of the game, strength, power and aggression all have their place. But the field of play is the only relevant context for aggression, and even there it must be controlled. It's too easy for players who step out of line off the field to give the game a bad name. The press will always be eager to latch on to any big name who falls foul of the law.

And it's also important to keep aggression under control. Then it can work in your favour. When it's out of control, it gives away penalties at best and sends you to the sin bin or even off the field at worst. Under control, aggression helps your side. Out of control, it's a liability.

So back to Leon Price and his first try. Earlier on I used Danny Brough's kicking ability to highlight the role of the cross-field high ball. In that case he kicked twice and both times his own winger gained possession, first to keep the move alive, then to score. Kevin Sinfield's was another example, but one where the high kick was spilled, providing an opportunity for Danny McGuire to score through the confusion. It's great when it works!

But kicker beware! You had better be accurate, get the flight, length and direction perfect. Because if you don't, the counter-attack will be quick and, just like an interception, it can be costly.

Back in 2000, Lyon Price is in a Bradford Bulls shirt facing St Helens in the play-offs. Saints are attacking on their left. A high kick goes up aimed at landing on or near the Bulls goal line. At least that seems to be the intention. But it's short, no more than five metres or so, but still short.

Leon Price takes the ball, turns and runs. He covers over 90 metres striding out in full flight and all the retreating defence can do is keep him away from the posts. The Saints players had all followed up the kick but, if anything, were ahead of it. So when Leon Price took the ball and set off, he had an open field ahead. It's a perfect example of how precise and accurate the cross-field kick has to be.

The second featured try is much more of a spectacle. I include it to show how Leon Price's combination of aggression, speed and strength can be an asset. But it also illustrates the use of the dummy in rugby league, because in one move there are three of them. Let's concentrate on the move rather than the players.

There's a play-the-ball wide on the St Helens left in the Grand Final against Hull, about 30 metres out. The ball goes right via two long passes to Leon Price.

The first pass from the dummy half is behind the player on the dummy run. It's a tactic that obviously confuses the markers in the defensive line.

Immediately there's a second pass to Leon Price and again it goes behind a dummy runner. With the ball in hand, Leon Price now throws a dummy of his own, but this time it's a dummy pass to his right. The Hull defender turns to anticipate the Saints player behind him receiving the ball. But, of course, it goes nowhere.

Price then is marked one-on-one. The power of the hand-off almost pushes him past the tackler. He's then in space and can take the diagonal towards the right corner to score. One move, three dummies, two dummy runs, one dummy pass.

Now there's a fine line between the legal and illegal on the dummy run. There was a time when the tactic would almost automatically have been penalised as obstruction. But this is yet another illustration of how technology has improved the game.

In such circumstances as the Leon Price try, the referee can always ask for the video to be checked to see if the defenders were impeded. If they were, of course, he gives a penalty. If they weren't, then it was a fair tactic, aimed at causing confusion.

46 – Chris Joynt

Superlatives often come easily. 'The best this' or 'the greatest that' can become everyday terms. But sometimes there is something that sticks out, something that continues to attract attention and comment alike. Standpoints that might usually differ sometimes come together to identify a truly iconic moment in the game, despite the fact that anyone who watches rugby league, or even has the slightest interest in it, surely has an opinion about the greatest try the game has ever seen.

There's one try that is so regularly listed among the all-time greats that it has to be a contender for the best ever. It was scored by one of the game's great professionals, a loyal servant of club and country. I refer to Chris Joynt, a player who gave St Helens 12 years of dedicated service.

It was a try that was enhanced even further by its importance. It wasn't scored in a cup final, nor a Grand Final, nor in a league leader's decider. It was scored in a Super League Championship play-off in front of a packed crowd and a huge television audience. But it's not purely because of setting and context that this try figures in my selection.

It was a try that won a game, secured progress in the play-offs, eventually led to a Saints triumph in the Grand Final and, on its own merits, entered rugby league folklore. But it was also a try scored by a player who made a habit of delivering both quality of product and quantity of effort. He was team captain that evening in 2000, as he was throughout six years from 1997 to 2003, years that were amongst the greatest in the club's history, a period when the club won four Super League titles, four Challenge Cups and a World Club Challenge.

This try, this great try was scored at the end of September 2000. In the game it brought Saints back from the dead. It also epitomised changes in the game that had begun with the professionalism of the Wigan team in the 1980s and 90s, a standard that was set and that others had to emulate. By the turn of the century, those necessary qualities had surely taken root throughout the game. But the try also illustrates again how fine is the line between success and failure.

At the end of September 2000, St Helens and Bradford Bulls are contesting a Championship play-off. Over 79 minutes have been played. The Bradford fans are counting down the seconds remaining on the clock, because their team is ahead by 11-10, their place in the next phase just one tackle away.

In rugby league, the only thing you can take for granted is that you can take nothing for granted. Anything can happen! If ever you need an example to illustrate this, then the 40 seconds it took St Helens to score this, perhaps most inventive and opportunistic of all tries in the game's history provides the perfect illustration. These 40 seconds, as it turns out, are like a novel. The try has a story. It seems long enough to have chapters, and here they are.

Chapter One

It's debatable whether there's any time left. The crowd is already counting down the clock when Paul Sculthorpe is tackled near the St Helens left touchline. Saints are 35 metres or so from their own line. There are just a few seconds left as Sculthorpe gets to his feet and plays the ball. Surely the game is over. The Bradford fans are ready to celebrate. The game is that close to its end. But Sculthorpe gets up and re-starts. There are seconds to go. We'll count the players as they touch the ball. Sculthorpe is number one. The acting half-back is number two. First receiver is Sean Long, player number three.

The clock has run out by now. But Saints have the ball in play and the game will not finish until the ball next goes dead. Bradford Bulls lead by 11-10. That's how close they are to going through.

Chapter Two

Sean Long decides to kick. But he kicks back towards his own line. In effect, it's a long cross-field pass to the right, along the St Helens line. It's a miss-pass with the boot. Hands number four, those of Kevin Iro, take the ball. He has to turn to take the kick. He's about 25 metres out, facing his own line. He turns again and delivers a pass to his right. Winger Steve Hall's hands are number five in the sequence.

Chapter Three

But the Bradford Bulls defence is well marshalled. The cover defence is aware of the danger and is in position. "Hall is trapped," said the match commentator, so the winger has to turn inside. Kevin Iro, his centre, has run ahead and is momentarily stranded beyond the play. So Steve Hall passes inside. The pass is made just to find a player. It's no more than speculative and prodding at this stage.

Hands number six are those of Sean Hoppe. And he is immediately faced with more Bradford defenders. He also has nowhere to go. His only option is to speculate even more. He throws a pass over his right shoulder, in the end a diagonal reverse pass thrown with speed on a loop. Did you catch that? Well, someone did. Hands number seven catch it and they're again Steve Hall's. He's stayed in support on the St Helens right after throwing his own pass just a moment earlier.

Hall now offloads quickly left to Tim Jonkers. Play is back in centre-field and Jonkers' hands are the eighth set to touch the ball. We're still operating near the St Helens 20-metre line, by the way. Play has actually gone back 15 metres or so from where we began.

Chapter Four

Jonkers now gives the ball to his left. Hands number nine belong to Sean Long. He made the original cross-field kick from ten metres or so further forward from where he receives this ball! I wonder whether in this story his character might have changed in the age it's taken for the ball to get back to him?

"Long fancies it," says Eddie Hemmings on Sky Television. He has time to say it twice before the Saints half-back releases. Saves money on scriptwriters, perhaps…

He makes a diagonal run towards the left touchline. Just as he reaches the spot where Sculthorpe originally played the ball, he's manufactured an opening. He's beaten off one tackle with speed and strength and then draws another before releasing the ball to the left a split second before the hit comes in. What he's done is not yet decisive, but it's been enough to create a weakness. This is chess at sprint pace, but there's time again for Eddie Hemmings to say things twice, as if the whole thing is actually in slow motion.

Chapter Five

Sean Long is able to pass to Dwayne West on the Saints left wing. His hands are the tenth St Helens pair in the move. "It's wide to West," came the commentary, twice. Wayne does a typical winger's job. He accelerates down the touchline side and beats two defenders with sheer speed and desire. You can't blame the Bradford defenders for missing tackles – they're tired and the game should be over. West outpaces and outstretches his opponents. They perform to their utmost, but it isn't enough. This score is no gift. In handing-off the first tackler West seems to gain extra momentum, enough to beat the second tackle, which seems to come in late. Perhaps it's late because of the push his teammate provided the winger. Now there's irony.

Chapter Six

West sprints over halfway. He has two Bradford Bulls defenders ahead. But crucially he has three St Helens teammates in close support just infield and two others in centre-field. That's five players who are effectively backing up. And there have already been ten sets of Saints hands on the ball!

Freeze the frame on the video and look at the Saints line. In overtime, after 80 gruelling minutes of a cup tie we are already eight passes into a move that has gone from extreme left to extreme right and back again, from 35 metres from the Saints line, back to 20 and then to ten metres inside the Bradford half. The move has done the width of the field twice, gone back nearly 20 metres and has just advanced by 40. And here are five Saints players – five! – in a perfectly staggered attacking line across half the width of the pitch. Now that's professionalism.

Chapter Seven

Pass number nine in the move, finding the eleventh pair of hands to touch the ball since the Sculthorpe play-the-ball, is timed to perfection. It goes to the winger's right, infield and finds Chris Joynt. Now remember that 80 minutes have already been played in a tough cup tie; tackling duties have been completed and captaincy has been another job to take for granted. It's almost a detail in this try to record that when Chris Joynt takes the ball, there are still 40 metres to go to the line – and there's a defender to be rounded along the way.

Chris Joynt covers that distance at a sprint, beats the defender with sheer pace and even has time to celebrate a little before instinctively heading in towards the posts, despite the fact that the kick is now academic, since play cannot continue and Saints have just won the game!

Chapter Eight - Postscript

At no point in this description of the Saints try have I mentioned the name of a Bradford player. No one missed a tackle. No one made a mistake. No one was found wanting. Yes, if luck had not been with St Helens that night, a kick would have been launched from the Sculthorpe play-the-ball, a Bradford player would have fielded and would have died with the ball. There would have been no overtime and St Helens would not have won the Grand Final that year against Wigan. The Bradford player taking that imagined kick, however, might have been criticised for dying with the ball.

When Saints won the same honour two years later, incidentally, it was by a single point, 19-18 again against Bradford Bulls. Controversially, a player called Chris Joynt collected a kick from Bradford Bulls in overtime, went to ground and was not penalised for a voluntary tackle, an offence that could have given a winning two points to Bradford via a penalty. What a game! What price success? And what price failure?

47 – Kyle Eastmond

When Shaun Edwards turned professional with Wigan, most pundits reckoned he would not take long to become established. His record at youth level was second to none. As ever, the only item of debate was his best position in the senior game. Unlike many players, Shaun kept people guessing about the answer to that question for most of his career!

I remember when Jason Robinson joined Wigan. At first he was to play at half-back. It was only after a few trial runs that he eventually settled in to the right wing position. And most of his England rugby union caps were later won as a fullback. Remember that in the early part of his career, Ellery Hanley was called a utility back, and he finished up a loose forward! The moral of this is that if you have natural talent for the game there are many places and ways you can express it on the field.

Occasionally however – perhaps no more than once in a lifetime – a player appears who seems to be made for a particular role, not by build or physical characteristics, but by a mixture of temperament, approach and skills. If anyone has emerged as a future power in the game in the last couple of years, then Kyle Eastmond has. And Kyle Eastmond will play at half-back.

Kyle is still only 20 years old. He's from Oldham, real rugby league heartland, and has been associated with St Helens since the age of 13. He now appears regularly in the first team as a graduate of the increasingly successful Saints academy.

These youth teams, in my opinion, are going to be the key to the development of the game in the next few years. Now that we have a period when there will be no relegation from Super League, clubs have a real opportunity to blood new talent and bring it on to the senior level.

And there are already some spectacular prospects out there. Richie Myler was unlucky – or perhaps lucky! – not to get a call-up for the 2008 World Cup. Sam Tomkins at Wigan is another young player with everything to play for. The third emergent half-back in this trio of talent is Kyle Eastmond. As we look forward to 2013, when these guys should be at the height of their careers, all we can say is that three into two doesn't go! So it's up to you, lads, to show what you can do. And, of course, a lot will depend on the success or otherwise of your respective clubs, so what happens in the head-to-head encounters between the clubs is going to have a big influence on future success for the individuals involved. Kyle Eastmond's talent is prodigious. There's a video on the internet of games he played at youth level for St Helens. I recommend you take a few minutes to watch it. You can see immediately the skills, talents and traits that are starting to become his trademark in Super League. He isn't the biggest man who ever played rugby league. But what a powerhouse he is! In these games for the youth team, play with the stop-start button when you've just seen Kyle Eastmond accelerate through a gap between two defenders. Stop the play, wind back and look at the situation before he made his move. Does it look like there's a gap? Then let the play progress and notice that the gap seems to appear only after he accelerates. His turn of pace is simply electric, far too quick for many defenders.

And what about the upper body strength? And the solidity of the footwork – and the sidestep – and the hand-off… Given Kyle Eastmond's skills, could you imagine him playing anywhere else but scrum-half or stand-off? Maybe he'll be a loose forward by the time he's 30! But I bet he'll have some trophies and a cabinet full of other honours by then!

Nothing sums up his abilities better than his winning try against Wigan at the end of July 2009. It's a wet night. The ball is slippery and players are skidding across the turf. There have been a few errors, one of which Kyle's competitor Sam Tomkins has pounced on to score a try. With three minutes left in the game, Wigan are ahead. And bear in mind the point I have made about the importance of head-to-head encounters in the future careers of these young players.

When Kyle Eastmond receives, he's centre-field, only a few metres out from the Wigan line. But there's a solid defence ahead. He has only a couple of strides with the ball before two tacklers close in. Now you have to watch this frame by frame, click by click to appreciate what goes on in this score.

Kyle anticipates the tackle, turns sideways towards the player, and puts his right shoulder into the guy's chest. At the same time, he digs a left arm hand-off into the second defender. These combined actions make the contacts of both tacklers less than perfect.

Kyle then gives a twist to the upper body. Did I mention upper body strength? And in an instant he's broken free. But by then he's almost stopped, his forward momentum absorbed in the contact. If there happened to be a Shaun Edwards passing by it would have been a perfect moment to offload to the player on the burst. But, that wet evening, Kyle Eastmond has just gone through a gap that didn't exist and so he's on his own.

He then seems to explode into a sprint. He doesn't accelerate. He switches on! He makes only four strides or so, moves a little right and immediately a bit more left as two more tacklers quickly close in.
His response? He stoops, dips as if diving forward, thus adding some gravity to his momentum. He has one tackler round his feet and another on his back as he goes to ground. But crucially he has three things in his favour. First, he has the conditions. He knows he will slide. Second, he has his forward momentum that he's preserved by leaning into the fall. Third, he has a free left arm with which, like a swimmer doing the crawl, he gives two rhythmic pushes against the turf.

He hits the ground a metre and a half short of the line carrying two defenders. But his ball-carrying hand makes no movement. Neither does his upper body as his left arm pushes two paces towards the score, which he makes under the posts to win the game. Watch carefully and there's even a suggestion that he's lifting himself and his tacklers clear of the ground with that left arm. And, by the way, he kicks goals as well! Now ask yourself, was there a gap before he accelerated?

Kyle Eastmond already seems to have understood what Shaun Edwards said to me those years ago. Pick your moment. Judge when the opportunity is good, and then take your chance. Then you'll convert a higher percentage of your chances into scores. Furthermore, the threat of a Kyle Eastmond break through the middle will prompt defensive lines to anticipate it, thus leaving gaps out wide that can be exploited as well. The whole team thus prospers from the individual ability – or even its threat – of a player like Kyle Eastmond, a player who certainly will continue to dominate the headlines.

By the time the 2013 World Cup comes round, players like Danny McGuire will be at the very top of their careers. Kyle Eastmond will be 24 or so. Would anyone like to bet now who will get the half-back places for England in that tournament? One thing is for sure. With players like Eastmond, Tomkins and Myler competing for places, the coming seasons are going to be nothing less than spectacular.

48 – Sean Long

It's ironic that I'm following a try by Kyle Eastmond with a piece about Sean Long. Sean Long is a player I've known since he first walked into the gym at Wigan nearly 15 years ago marked for stardom. And now after 12 years at St Helens, Sean Long moves on at the end of the season to Hull on a two-year contract. He says that he's looking forward to the challenge, believing that the role he'll play for his new club will revitalise his career.

I know what it feels like to leave a winning side. In the

1990s, Wigan were the team of the decade. After they lost that mantle, really when Super League began, St Helens took it up. Sean Long joined Saints in 1997 and, since then, the list of honours they have won is just remarkable. And Sean Long has been the club's lynchpin throughout.

No other player in the history of the game has won three Lance Todd Trophies. Perhaps no other player in modern times has won a game so often through individual brilliance. But, in Sean Long's case, that outstanding talent rarely shows up as a length-of-the-field sprint for a try, or even a power-house drive over from close range. Sean Long's game is pure stealth, built on fitness and unending hard work, of course, but it's pure stealth that he's used consistently over the years to win games. So, in Sean's case, my *50 Of The Best* is not going to feature any of the more than 150 tries he's scored in over 300 appearances for Saints. Neither is it going to describe any of the more than 1,000 goals he's kicked. Sean Long, as you will see later, seems to put teamwork at the top of his own list of priorities. So, for his entry in my *50 Of The Best*, I am going to feature his role as provider.

Sean Long and I go back a long way. I first met him when he was very young, still in the academy at Wigan. He was Wigan-born and, above all else, he wanted to play for his home town club. I played alongside him when he made his debut against Hull. He set me up for a try. It's as if that act of providing a try for me set the pattern for Sean's entire career. So, from day one, the strength of Sean's game was what he could do to create opportunities for others.

I've always felt that I've got a talent for spotting players who are going to make a mark on the game. In Sean's case, I knew that he was going to be a great player from the minute I saw him.

Now, when I played for Wigan, I didn't knock about much with my teammates because I used to live in Manchester. The older players, most of whom lived near Wigan, used to go home at lunchtime, but I used to stay on. The academy lads, of course, were still there because theirs was a full-time job and they had to stay all day doing odd jobs. As a result, I got to know quite a lot of the young players of the time, such as Simon Haughton and Kris Radlinksi. Longey was another of them around that time and he certainly stood out.

I can remember meeting him one day during the extra time that I used to do in the gym during those afternoons. I knew he was talented, but at that time his temperament wasn't right. He had to mature. The club insisted, for instance, that the lads got an all-round education in case they didn't make it in the game. It made perfect sense, but not to Sean, who thought it was a waste of time.

When Wigan let him go, I think he was completely shattered at first. Later, maybe, it accomplished two things. One, it made him more determined to succeed when a good opportunity came along, and two, it made him play out of his skin whenever Saints met Wigan. In my opinion, if Saints decide to put up a statue of anyone outside their ground, it ought to be one of Sean Long. He's been at the top of the game for a decade and a consistent performer throughout. Despite the fact that he rarely scores spectacular tries, we can all remember occasions when Sean Long has won the game for St Helens. How many times can we remember a one point victory for Saints following a late drop goal by Longey? You can include two Grand Finals and one World Club Challenge in the list! There have been crucial passes to find a player in space, a winger with an overlap, or a player inside on the burst. Sean Long has been the complete play-maker for Saints. But he's now 32 and both club and player are aware that all good things have to come to an end. One thing is for sure, Sean's professionalism and love of the game will mean that he'll give nothing less than one hundred per cent for his new club in the next two seasons.

So which aspect of Sean Long's game should I feature? Well, it's something I've highlighted already in my *50 Of The Best*. It's his cross-field kick to the wing. I featured Kevin Sinfield's kick for Leeds that Danny McGuire converted into a try. But that only happened after Danny himself produced some individual brilliance after the ball went loose. I highlighted Danny Brough's two cross-field kicks in one move for Wakefield Trinity that led to a Scott Grix try. But it was only after a lucky rebound from the first kick that the move progressed.

In Sean Long's case, I'm going to feature his performance in the 2006 Grand Final against Hull. In the end, St Helens ran out comfortable winners, but two tries came directly from Sean Long kicks. When you watch the video, it's hard to imagine what you could have done to defend against such accuracy.

There was one in each half. The first helped open the scoring for St Helens after Hull had almost taken the lead. The kick from Long was a delicate chip. He was about 20 metres from the Hull line, with the ball going left. The Hull defensive line was well forward, making a pass risky, but leaving space behind. He chose the diagonal towards the left corner, with the ball bouncing once infield before crossing the try-line. Francis Meli, the Saints left wing, was first there and could take the ball and dive to score in one movement. The kick's placement was so perfect that only – I stress only – Francis Meli could have got to it. No Hull defender was even in the race.

If the first was short and delicate, the second was high and long. It was after 53 minutes of the game that Sean Long made his second try-scoring kick. Play was again about 20 metres from the Hull line, and again on the St Helens left. Long's kick this time, however, was cross-field, high and travelling over two thirds of the width of the field. It was flighted to drop right on the Hull goal line near the right corner. As is often the case with such kicks, the defender has to wait while the attacking player sprints forward. In the jump for the ball, the defender's standing start is always going to be second best. In this case, Saints' right wing, Ade Gardner, gets up to take the ball. To score, because of the accuracy of the kick, all he has to do next is fall down.

That year, 2006, was a special season for St Helens. The team and its captain, Sean Long, lifted all three major trophies – the League Leadership, Challenge Cup and Grand Final. Sean Long also won the Lance Todd

Trophy for himself that year. Bradford Bulls had done it in 2003, but since 1997 Saints have lifted the Grand Final trophy four times and finished league leaders five times. On top of that, they've won the Challenge Cup six times. They've lifted the World Club Challenge twice and been runners-up twice. No other team has a record to match and few other players currently in Super League come close to matching Sean Long's individual consistency, staying power and ability to create scoring opportunities.

When asked at the end of the 2006 Grand Final what had been the key to the St Helens success that night, Sean Long, having created two tries with cross-field kicks, replied, "Our defence – it always is."

49 – Gene Miles

I want to pick up on three themes from the Sean Long piece – doing the treble, being a provider and the importance of defence. For me, these three things bring back memories of a player who occupies a special place in my rugby league career, a player from whom I learned a lot in the relatively short time we played together. As a direct result of his unique skills I enjoyed perhaps the best spell of all my years in the game.

The St Helens side of 2006 was all-conquering, completing the treble success of lifting the League Leadership, the Grand Final and the Challenge Cup. In 1991-92, my first season at Central Park, Wigan did the same, except in those days the names were slightly different, being the Challenge Cup,

Championship and Premiership.

It was quite a season for the club and, had I not scored that Wembley try in 1994, could easily have been the high point of my career. I'd already had good times and considerable success with Widnes, but that first season at Wigan was like living a dream. In the cup semi-final that year, we scored over 70 points against Bradford and over 40 against St Helens in the play-off final. And a lot of those points came from me! In the Challenge cup semi-final against Bradford, I scored five tries and in the play-off semi-final against Leeds, I scored ten. I got a 50-metre gem in the match against Saints, and that was the year that I really scored a hat-trick against Castleford at Wembley, despite the record books listing the three as two scored and one knocked-on! It doesn't get much better than that for a rugby league player.

I admit that I did quite well at Wigan when it came to centres, however. I had a good relationship with Gary Connolly, for instance. Gary, as we know, was a talented player in many positions and for several clubs, a real servant of the game. Andrew Farrar before him was a bit of a let-down for me, because he had a tendency to cut inside. But, to continue the reverse order in time, anything would have been a comedown from what had gone before. In my first season at Wigan I had the privilege – nothing less than privilege – of playing outside one of the greatest centres the game has ever seen. I'm talking, of course, about Gene Miles.

Gene was a complete giant of a man. I've turned out alongside bigger players but none whose presence was so intimidating. He was pretty much at the end of his career by the time he came to Wigan. For a couple of seasons before he arrived, he had even been playing in the second row. He'd captained the Brisbane Broncos and been capped 14 times for Australia, but had announced his retirement from international rugby a couple of seasons before so that he could concentrate on his club commitments.

I remember he would often take things easy in training, allowing me to go inside to the centre while he ambled up and down the wing. But when it came to the day of the match, there was no one more focused, committed or completely professional.

His knack of drawing in a crowd of tacklers and then offloading the ball one-handed was uncanny. A lot of it was pure strength, of course, but he also had amazing skill, great positional play and superb timing. He was also completely unselfish. With Gene Miles in a Wigan shirt we won the lot. We even won the World Sevens that year, beating his old club Brisbane in the final. Now anyone who has played a sevens tournament will know that it can be a non-stop, exhausting experience, so you can see he was no sloucher!

Gene was originally scheduled to play two seasons with Wigan, but it turned out to be just one. He played just 29 games for the club, but the partnership he and I forged that season has become legendary. Basically, the club couldn't afford him. He'd stated his terms and the club couldn't meet them.

I have to admit to shedding a tear or two when I was told he wasn't coming back, especially when the new face proved to be a clear second best. No one – and I stress no one – I've ever played alongside was as good as Gene Miles at unselfishly setting up opportunities for his winger. As often happens in team games, it's the player who scores the try or who nets the goal that gets a name on the score sheet and an entry in the record books. But often, certainly in the cases of Sean Long and Gene Miles, it's the provider that actually makes the score. Do you remember, incidentally, Gary Schofield's comment about being tossed around like a rag doll by Mal Meninga? Well, that's what Brian Noble said about Gene Miles after our cup semi-final trouncing of Bradford. So, a triple for Wigan and the role of Gene Miles as provider are two of my three links with the Sean Long piece. The third, defence, arises out of the Gene Miles try I've chosen to include in my *50 Of The Best*.

Gene scored many tries, mostly using his most recognisable trademark: his power and strength. You'll see many of his scores completed with tacklers on his back, hanging on to his legs, piling on top as he goes over the line.

But the try I've chosen is presented more for what it illustrates about the game than its spectacle. The context in which it's scored is crucial, as is the way it's executed. It certainly highlights the fact that defensive skills can and do win matches. Or should I say that the lack of them loses matches?

Gene Miles came on two tours to England. He was a

member of the 1982 *Invincibles* but didn't play in the tests. He'd only been in the game just over one season at the time. By next time round, however, he was number one choice at left centre. And he scored a memorable try, perhaps not a great try in itself, but certainly a significant one against Great Britain. It's a try that perhaps underlines the key difference between the sides – the defensive consistency of the Kangaroos married to clinical finishing in attack, versus the inconsistent Great Britain defence alongside occasional attacking flair. Remember that last-minute Old Trafford try by Mal Meninga a few years later? It could and perhaps should have been stopped well before Stuart broke clear. This Gene Miles try is much simpler, but it illustrates similar issues. In terms of points scored it was just as effective as any length-of-the-field spectacular.

It's the First Test at Old Trafford in 1986. We're 20 metres out from the Great Britain line with Australia in possession. Wally Lewis receives. The match commentator describes him as stepping and weaving. Basically he's doing something similar to what I've claimed for Kyle Eastmond. He's using a combination of hand-off, shoulder and upper body strength to break free of tacklers. But he seems to find the task less than troublesome! He's clearly more interested in creating enough space to pass than making a clean break. In this case, however, you have to think that the defenders ought to be able to smother the ball and prevent the offload.

But they don't. Lewis is centre-field and is able to break free from the defenders long enough to feed a short pass to his right. Gene Miles is coming through at speed.

Ellery Hanley, playing at centre that day, scampers across to cover, but the big man uses his power and is unstoppable. He grounds by the posts. And that's how defences can win matches – or lose them. It's as quick as that! Oh, by the way, Gene Miles scored three that day!

Like the *Invincibles*, the 1986 Australian tourists also went through their schedule of games unbeaten. They adopted the title the *Unbeatables,* and perhaps have not received the accolades they deserve compared to their countrymen of four years earlier. It always helps to be first in anything! But don't underestimate for one moment how good this team was and don't for one second forget the pivotal role that Gene Miles played in it.

But what is so impressive about Gene Miles, a fact that came home to me in my first dream season at Wigan, was his complete unselfishness. I'd already scored more than 180 tries for Widnes and played outside some wonderful centres – and there was none better than the lanky Darren Wright. But I know that if Gene Miles had played a second season for Wigan then, barring injury, I would have reached my target of 500 career tries at least one season earlier!

50 – Wally Lewis

Now you all know that I was brought up in London, well away from rugby league's heartland. All the rugby I played in my youth was rugby union. You probably also know that I went to a boarding school and that, before I signed for Widnes, I knew next to nothing about rugby league. It's perhaps because of such things that I've never really felt wholly accepted into rugby league's world. Nowadays it doesn't worry me. The fact is that I'm the British game's third greatest ever try-scorer – and the only player in the modern game to come anywhere near records that are nearing 50 years old. The idea that this is sometimes still not recognised by some associated with the game is just laughable. But there was a time when I wondered what I could do to feel more on the inside. I can remember in my early days at Widnes, when I felt I already knew how to run up and down a touchline, asking my teammates who they thought was the best player in the world. They all said the same name: Wally Lewis. I, of course, being from London, burst out laughing.

Where I grew up, a wally was an idiot! It's not a nasty term of abuse, but it's dismissive. You'll understand why I laughed when they mentioned the name. Believe me, I stopped laughing the moment I saw Wally Lewis play. To describe his talent as awesome is a complete understatement. Too many fans of the game in Britain – except at Wakefield Trinity for whom he played ten games in 1983-4 – regard him as a manipulator, as a player who was lucky far too often, a player who never got the comeuppance he deserved. They are wrong, of course. In Wally Lewis's case, it wasn't luck that went his way, it was talent.

Wally Lewis has been described – and not just once, and not just from within rugby league – as the greatest rugby player of all time, from any country, from any form of the game. And don't forget that he was a youth international for Australia in rugby union, touring Europe and Japan with teammates such as Mark Ella and Michael O'Connor. It's interesting to note that of these three names, one played only league and one only union, while the other crossed codes.

It's probably not easy for people based in the United Kingdom to understand that the rugby union versus rugby league divide was not restricted to within our shores. Wally Lewis started playing rugby when he was six, and because his family was a league family – his father was a professional with two Brisbane clubs – that's the code he eventually played. After representing his country in union at youth level, he felt he was being discriminated against because of his league background and so turned his back on that code. He didn't turn his back on his home state, Queensland, however. He never did, despite lucrative offers over the years from Sydney clubs. His ten matches with Wakefield Trinity were his only foray outside of his home state, apart from tours with the Kangaroos.

Now one player doesn't make a team. We've seen repeatedly in this *50 Of The Best* how teamwork is always essential. But in Wally Lewis's case, his individual presence and its ability to motivate players was prodigious. In the ten games he had with Wakefield, they won five. When he left, they lost every game through to the season end and were relegated. He might not have set the place alight, but he had massive influence.

The man's record is amazing. His career spanned 14 seasons from 1978 to 1992. He made his international debut in 1981. He was vice-captain of the *Invincibles* in 1982, though controversially the selectors preferred Brett Kenny for the tests. He captained the 1986 *Unbeatables* and was national team captain for five years until 1989, winning 33 caps. Let's understate something: he won a World Cup! He played 31 State of Origin games, 30 as captain of Queensland and was a record eight times man of the match. He has a statue in bronze outside Lang Park, Brisbane, where he's known as the Emperor, his more mundane title being the King, King Wally.

So what was it about Wally Lewis's game that made him so special? He did score tries from long range, occasionally. But his ball distribution was quite incredible. He was one of the toughest tacklers in the game. He was ruthless when presented with a chance. His kicking game was almost undoubtedly the best ever. And, when it came to teamwork, he was unselfish, always watching for the best way for his team to exploit an advantage.

In a nutshell he had a great brain, a rugby brain, the one thing that unites most who I've mentioned in this book. Without it you're nothing. We've all seen great athletes attempt to play this game of ours, but the basic questions are can they play, do they have a rugby brain? Skill and athleticism won't make you a great player without a rugby brain and King Wally had the ultimate.

The try I've chosen here is again from that game in 1988,

Australia versus Great Britain in Sydney. It's a try that perfectly sums up Wally Lewis's game and his uncompromising approach. At first sight, it may not seem spectacular until you look at it frame by frame to see what's going on.

Great Britain have done well. We're into the second half and still hold the lead. Those two first half tries, my own and Phil Ford's, plus the conversion were still the difference between the teams. Australia badly need a score to get back into the game.

Wally Lewis provides them with a good position via a kick to touch, down the right. Australia take the scrum at the second attempt against head and feed. They play a couple of drives diagonally to the left. Second row, Paul Vautin, 'Fatty' to his friends, has reached the ten-metre line, just left of the posts. Hooker Gary Conescu is dummy half.

Now on this play, watch Conescu a few times. Wind the action back and forth while Vautin is getting up to play the ball. Once, twice, three times, no less than four times Conescu looks across to his right. Four times he looks at Lewis so he can deliver what his captain wants. The tacklers on Vautin were Paul and David, the brothers Hulme. Paul gets up and rejoins the defensive line in front of the Great Britain posts.

When the ball is played, Lewis takes the pass from Conescu. Lewis is on the burst, but not, you might think, at full pelt. His style was always deceptive. Watch other videos of his play when he appears to be ambling. And then ask yourself who's catching him up? Answer: probably no one!

The pass from Conescu is so short he almost hands Lewis the ball. He's just ten metres for the try-line, angling right towards the posts.

He meets a tackle from Paul Hulme at five metres. It looks a pretty good tackle. Hulme is round Lewis's hips and has a good hold. Surely the tackle has halted the progress.

But watch Lewis shrug off the contact as fullback Phil Ford arrives to join in. As Ford approaches, Lewis offers him a hand-off with his left hand and then turns, shows him his back. Peter Jackson, left centre, approaches. Will Lewis slip the ball? Conescu approaches. Will he offload?

All the time look at the base Lewis has given himself. His tree-trunk legs are wide apart, locked at the knee. His upper body has two tacklers in contact, but he still stands up.

What he then does is unclear, even a frame at a time. He seems to duck under the tackle and, in the same movement, he turns back towards the line and dips. As players of both sides join what is nearly a ruck, Lewis grounds the ball for a try. Neither his feet nor his body ever reach the try-line. He doesn't go to ground, indeed it seems that he remains upright throughout. And yet he grounds the ball.

Think back to how Lewis put Gene Miles in for a try at Old Trafford. Then have a look at how many times you can find videos of Lewis himself scoring from close range with a tackler on his back, another swinging round a leg and another round his neck.

If a player can score such tries at all, it's a talent. To do it regularly and consistently, even when the opposition is expecting it, is a prodigious skill. And in this featured try, if Wally Lewis had not gone it alone, he could have used either of the two opportunities to offload he'd created along the way! He was quite simply the best rugby player of all time, in any country, in any code.

In my introduction to this selection of tries, I mentioned five aspects of the game, strength, speed, tactics, teamwork and stealth, and have used them to label aspects of particular plays. In this try by Wally Lewis, a try that at first sight might not appear too spectacular, we have all five elements in equal measure. His speed always was deceptive, while his strength was awesome. He took this ball on the burst and his tacklers couldn't knock him off his feet. It took four consultations with Conecsu at the play-the-ball to identify the pass he wanted. His teammates, knowing his ability to offload in almost any situation, backed up in numbers, though in this case the teamwork was used as a grand decoy. And the whole thing is the very quintessence of stealth!

In the 1988 Third Test in Sydney, the efforts of Wally Lewis and his teammates were not enough because Great Britain ran out winners. Over the years, however, the record speaks for itself. I'm in no way suggesting that it's all down to one man, but if ever you wanted someone to symbolise ability and achievement in the game, Wally Lewis would be your man. In Australia, he's officially known as an *Immortal*!

But no one is immortal. Wally Lewis lost the captaincy of the Brisbane Broncos to Gene Miles and, though he played a couple of seasons at loose forward when his pace started to wane, he finally retired from the game in 1992.

In recent years, Wally Lewis has devoted much of his time and effort to charity work. His daughter was born profoundly deaf and he's supported the work of charities dedicated to assisting those with similar conditions.

He's also undergone brain surgery to alleviate his own epilepsy and has made a complete recovery. He kept his condition quiet over the years and coped with its consequences throughout his playing career. One of those consequences, it seems, is that he has no personal recollection of many of the great moments in his career. Thank goodness for the videos! Not at all bad, for a Wally!

Future

Rugby league is a fundamentally honest and law-abiding sport. For people outside the game, that statement might seem ironic, or prompt expressions of disbelief. And if all I had from rugby league were teenage memories of Hull Kingston Rovers players apparently bathing in mud on BBC Television's Saturday afternoon Grandstand, then I might also be amongst the surprised. If what you see of the game is only so-called highlights featuring high tackles, hits or foul play, then you also might not agree.

Many people outside the game associate rugby league with the televised mass brawl. We've all seen them. The apparently uncontrolled punch-ups, usually involving forwards around a scrum in a game whose passions have overflowed. The referee, often a small man, stands aside while mayhem seems to rule. I've even heard past commentators from rugby union express an opinion that the very name rugby league was synonymous with violence.

Rugby league, like union, is a passionate sport. Some players work themselves up into an aggressive frenzy in the dressing room before the game. I won't go into what is sometimes said or more usually shouted on such occasions, because I want to preserve this book's universal certificate! If you feel you'd like to criticise this practice, I suggest you imagine the frame of mind you, the reader, would personally have to adopt if you found yourself standing on the right wing at Odsal

Stadium, Bradford, with 105 kilograms of Lesley Vainikolo ahead, running straight at you at 35 kilometres per hour. Any sensible human being would probably get out of the way. That means rugby league players must be less than sensible, because they throw themselves at him into the equivalent of a low-speed car crash. Then they get up and do it all over again for 80 minutes and repeat, every week for half a year so that audiences, both in the ground and on television, can have their spectacle.

In saying that rugby league is, as I say, a fundamentally honest game I'm not claiming that players never breach the laws of the game. Neither am I denying that rules are regularly bent, even pushed to their limits in search of that crucial advantage. I recognise that players sometimes lose their temper, can be guilty of foul play and occasionally do some things on the pitch that might put them in jail if they happened on the street. And, all this probably applies to rugby as a whole.

Rugby league, however, has an assumption amongst all involved in the game that foul play will be identified and punished, that rule-breaking will be discovered, that suitable sanctions and penalties will be applied and that these will be accepted by the recipients. There's always room for discussion, but out-and-out argument or dissent, a failure to accept a decision, or not retreating immediately after being penalised will receive immediate further punishment. Everyone knows it and, if the punishment comes, everyone accepts it.

A perfect example of how honesty amongst rugby league players tends to be assumed is the reaction of those who witnessed England's encounter with New Zealand in the last World Cup. New Zealand had fought back to wipe out an early deficit. I won't make any comment on the play or how the game developed. What I will say is that New Zealand first took the lead in the second half when Issac Luke kicked a penalty. He'd already played a big part in the New Zealand revival after coming on as an interchange.

The problem was that the penalty was awarded for an obstruction on Issac Luke after he'd played a short chip kick. It was widely reported and commented upon at the time that his ploy was a fake, a dive that succeeded in tricking the referee.

Now, I'm in no way suggesting that this score or alleged act of foul play was in itself instrumental in bringing about England's defeat, because the eventual scoreline showed a fairly comfortable win for New Zealand. What I am saying is that the universal reference to its questionable honesty shows just how straight the game is expected to be. And, if I remember correctly, the response of the New Zealand bench that evening was to bring the player off the field. Whether this was to punish him or protect him, only they know. When did you last see a footballer substituted because he'd taken a dive?

One of the strengths of rugby league is its ability to confront difficult issues and to find solutions. And if those solutions prove to be not quite perfect, they are evaluated and modified. If football, for instance, allowed a physio onto the pitch without having to stop the game, the seriousness or otherwise of an injury could be quickly assessed and a signal sent to the referee to blow the whistle. If the injury was not serious, it could be treated immediately, as in league. If play were to drift back towards the injured player, the referee would still have the right to stop the game at any point. And what about allowing immediate interchange as in league, an interchange that can be reversed at any time, to avoid a team being a man down? It's different in football, perhaps, but I'm sure that this example highlights some of the strengths of league.

When I read recent criticism of the results of video referee deliberations, I like to remind myself of how often they get it right. When there was just one perspective on a decision, there were obviously some mistakes. To insist on retaining just one perspective, when crowds and television viewers have access to replays, analysis and software to predict the flight of a ball is, frankly, stupid. It can do nothing more than bring a game into disrepute if it continues to allow results to hinge on errors that can and should be avoided. And criticism that the system cannot be totally accurate can be easily countered. Having technology gets the accuracy closer to one hundred per cent than not having it! In addition, you can build your own fudge factor into the system by retaining a 'benefit of the doubt' option in favour of the scorer if there's simply insufficient evidence to make a decision. Now I wonder which sport already has that!

Personally, I'd like to see an extension of the use of video evidence in disciplinary matters, especially involving any aspect of deliberate foul play, rather than technicalities. This couldn't be done during the game, of course, but sanctions could be applied after the game, if the referee and assistants had missed a serious misdemeanour. And what's more I think that as a sport we should publicise what we do and how we use the systems to demonstrate that the game is both honest and open, and that we're determined to keep it that way. It's a system that's working and we can make it work both better and faster to further improve the game.

Make no mistake, the outcomes of these decisions can change careers, even a player's entire life. The story I've described arising out of Ken Hirst's try in the 1968 Challenge Cup Final is only one illustration, though, in that instance a video referee would probably have upheld all the contentious decisions in the game, apart from the decision to play it!

Just take a moment to imagine how my own career or the entire game's development might have differed if a video referee had been in place in 1995! There am I, acting half back, I recall – didn't I say earlier that I always fancied myself as a ball distributor? – and then on the break. Steve Menzies tries to catch me. I think it was Tim Brasher who tried to cut me up into touch, so I throw the ball inside where Paul Newlove is backing up. He takes the pass and scores. It all comes to nothing because the touch judge has his flag up, saying that I stepped on the line before releasing. Fine. That was his judgement, and that judgement has to be made in a split second.

But when the incident was viewed on the replay, my foot wasn't on the line. I wasn't in touch. That try was good and should not have been disallowed. The game? The 1995 World Cup Final, of course, England versus Australia at Wembley. That score would have put us ahead. Now this is the main reason why I included my 1988 score against Australia in Sydney. It was the opening score in that game. It put us ahead. It was a confidence-boosting effort achieved through teamwork. It gave us a good start and a platform from which we could go on to win. If there had been a video referee in the 1995 World Cup Final, England would have had a similar start. What a difference to the sport an England win in the game's centenary year might have made. To say that rugby league is sometimes a game of inches is an overstatement – millimetres might be closer!

In this example, no player is at fault. No one tried to cheat. There was no deliberate attempt to alter the course of the game. There was no foul play. An official, charged with the responsibility of making a decision, carried out that responsibility to the best of his ability. But play had progressed beyond the limits of his accuracy. He had to make a call, and he may have got it wrong. Given that player who took the pass went on to score, who could possibly object to the use of video evidence to check its legality?

And let's not forget that the introduction of the video referee was basically a Sky TV, Super League initiative. It illustrates how a sport can have a symbiotic relationship with its prime broadcast medium. The two relate to one another, even depend on one another, so why not do more than merely co-exist? Why not cooperate and work together to enhance the quality of the experience for everyone? Accusations that the sport only exists in the pocket of the media interest are irrelevant. In our era, that dependency would apply no matter what kind of direct relationship existed.

Now it may be that the relationship won't be permanent, because nothing in sport – or even life, for that matter! – ever is. But the development of this relationship is another example of how rugby league has the ability to re-invent itself a little at a time, always keeping the improvement of its spectators' experience as its prime goal.

And talking of spectators, I want to take this opportunity to pay tribute to the contribution made to the game by Eddie Hemmings and Mike Stephenson. They were pioneers of the modern game's coverage and over the years have become institutions in their own right. Stevo's T-R-Y has become rugby league's iconic catchphrase. And I also want to recognise the contribution of Neville Smith, executive producer of rugby league for Sky Sports. Fans of the game might not be aware of the immense contribution such people make behind the scenes. The close relationship between television and the sport's administrators again illustrates the fact the rugby league has always been willing, more willing than in most sports, to consider issues, evaluate options and then make decisions. If this now also incorporates the interests of the broadcaster, then so be it. The audience is now bigger than those who've paid at the turnstiles, so needs to be considered and catered for.

If video referees have been one innovation that has

grown out of rugby league's special relationship with television, then the summer game has been another. Becoming a summer contact sport was a good move. Rugby league is all about speed and teamwork, and both running and handling are helped by summertime's generally harder – sometimes even drier! – pitches. The days of the Grandstand winter mud bath are gone for good. The move to the summer has thus been a complete success, because it has stressed and then enhanced the game's existing strengths.

A more recent and more interesting change has been the suspension of promotion and relegation for a full three seasons. Participation in Super League is now via a licence awarded by the sport's governing body. This brings the European Super League closer into line with the Australian game, itself modelling characteristics imported from the organisational structures of sport in the United States. It's a system that has some obvious benefits and some other equally obvious problems. Starting with the latter, one consequence is that some of rugby league's most famous clubs will have no prospect of promotion, and thus no prospect of participating in Super League. I spent four highly successful years with Widnes and it's a shame that they aren't part of the top flight. But then neither is Featherstone, or Halifax, or Leigh. Great names from the game's past, such as Oldham and Swinton and Hunslet aren't in the frame. And then let's not forget Doncaster, York, Dewsbury, Batley, Keighley, Bramley, Blackpool and Liverpool-Huyton. And of course, we always used to forget about Whitehaven and Workington, even when they were thoroughly part of the game's traditional heartland! I'm sure that Rochdale Hornets were in there somewhere! And yet there's the point. Neither is Broughton Rangers, Brighouse Rangers, Liversedge or Manningham or Tyldesley, not to mention Runcorn or Stockport! The game has changed, and some tradition always has to go to make way for something new.

A Super League licence, however, does not mean a club has a guaranteed presence. The licence lasts for three years, but in exceptional circumstances it can be revoked, in which case a replacement might have to be found. After all, there is always the possibility of managerial or financial meltdown that might prompt intervention.

The absence of promotion and relegation might have removed some of the targets for the Co-Operative Championship clubs. But for Super League teams it has provided stability designed to help them both change and develop. With relegation threatening, the temptation to bring in imported talent to get a quick fix in the form of a few league points always won out over longer-term and undoubtedly more important investment. If your youth teams are being well coached and their talent nurtured, you'll generate a supply of players ready to join Super League and able to meet its standards. They'll stay at your club if you've been sufficiently successful and can offer them the right terms. Otherwise, of course, they'll look elsewhere.

But it takes a number of years to develop youth programmes. And young people don't grow up any faster as a result of changing your methods. It can take years to reform existing systems that aren't delivering. It also takes resources. If a short-term goal of avoiding relegation is around, that's always going to take precedence. Under a three-year licensing system, the task can at least begin in those clubs where it's been neglected and can be consolidated and improved where it's already underway. I reckon that's good future thinking.

I sense that the game is currently rejuvenating itself from within, from the bottom up. Products from the more successful youth programmes are already in the game. And there are some very promising talents emerging. We can only look forward with anticipation to the time when more teams have highly successful programmes and a new generation of young players, wholly raised within the professional outfits, emerges.

There's no intended criticism here for what went on in the past. But, just as in the mid-1990s Wigan led the way towards a fully professional sport at senior level, perhaps St Helens has led the way in recent years in creating a youth academy to support its senior professional outfit. What three-year licences provide is the opportunity for all clubs to reform their own structures in the same way they had to do in relation to their first team squad after the creation of Super League.

But if Super League sides are to retain this home-grown talent, they'll have to succeed on the pitch as well and it's obvious that not everyone can be a winner. What would look healthier for rugby league as a whole would be an indication that honours in the different competitions were being shared around a little more. It would indicate that overall standards throughout were on the rise. For me it was good to be part of Wigan's dominance of rugby league in the first half of the 1990s, but it perhaps wasn't so good for the game as a whole. At the time, as I've said, Wigan were in a different league. It wasn't that we were always the better team, but we were always more professional and often that, in itself, saw us through.

The licensing system is an attempt to ensure that all sides participating in Super League satisfy certain essential criteria. It's also a vehicle for encouraging best practice where that has generated beneficial results. If the result of the system is the creation of a league that's keenly contested, where games are both hard-fought and close, and where the results are unpredictable, then it will have succeeded. If not, it will no doubt be the criteria that are amended and not the system itself. I've a feeling that licensing is here to stay, but I'm sure there's nothing magic about the number 14. I predict it will expand.

The big threat to Super League at the moment is the quality of its facilities. The award by the Super League of A, B or C status to the licences is, for me, mainly linked to stadium quality and spectator facilities. We might recall great moments associated with names such as Watersheddings, Thrum Hall, Barley Mow, Parkside, The Boulevard and Belle Vue. Venues come and go, and some of them stay. Then there was Craven Park and Central Park. Spell-checkers will be happy that Fartown disappeared!

But we mustn't let nostalgia carry us away into a romanticised version of the past. I'd bet that current crowds at the JJB Stadium still lament the passing of Central Park. I also bet they wouldn't be so charitable if they still had to go there!

The old Odsal was enormous, but it had no permanent terracing. Now, as the Gratton Stadium, it offers a complete spectator experience, including a pre-match show. Things have changed, and things are going to change in many of the older grounds as well. Some years ago, when new guidelines were introduced for football stadiums, Premiership teams had to upgrade. Super League licences aim to effect the same kind of changes in rugby league and spectators will benefit.

Super League teams now have a clear responsibility – even duty – to ensure that requested upgrades to their stadiums are either underway or past the planning stage by the time the next licences are awarded in 2011. Money is short, we all know that. But the agenda has been tabled and now it's up to management to do its job. Super League teams of the future will have to be well run in every aspect. The team will have to perform to acceptable standards on the pitch, the commercial side will have to be both viable and visionary, and links to youth and community will have to be vibrant and effective.

But, there's another aspect to management, one that will play a bigger role in the game's future. Increasingly, the affairs of players entering the game are being handled by agents and advisers. In the game's semi-professional era, players were very much on their own. When I joined Widnes in 1987, I was a full-time professional sportsman. But a number of my teammates weren't. I had to figure out a lot of things for myself. There was no support network or financial advice around. There was no one doing the kind of job that I now do on behalf of players. There were the team coaches, of course, to advise on what to do on the field, but there was no advice on contracts, lifestyle, nutrition or health or how to be a professional. I found out for myself what I should or shouldn't eat and made up my own mind not to drink alcohol. I was pretty disciplined and focused. Had I not been, my career wouldn't have progressed as it did.

But now, two decades on, we have a whole academic discipline of sports science that has research findings on many aspects of performance enhancement. Keeping up with new findings is a job in itself, not something that a professional sportsman can do alongside the day job. But advisers can do it and in the future will increasingly pass on both advice and good practice to the players they manage. By the time new licences are granted in 2011, I expect most players to operate under such a system.

As a result, we can expect some lengthy and complex, but perhaps more professionally conducted contract negotiations in the coming years. Whether they might lead to some players securing commitments across codes, like I did with London Broncos and Bedford, however, remains to be seen. Personally, I think that if a player was any good, there would be increased pressure from one side or the other for a higher level of commitment. And that would have to be addressed. If the player wasn't outstanding, then the option might not be available.

So where does all this take us? Well, first we have in Super League a vibrant, popular sport with a loyal following. It's made for television and audiences are good. It's made great progress towards extending its base, but there's more work to do. The game has expanded at every other level and continues to do so. In fact, rugby league is now played in every English county. Some recent graduates from the academies have joined the senior game and are nothing less than exceptional prospects. And I'm sure there are more in the pipeline.

A number of Super League grounds will have to be upgraded. A shortage of finance coupled with, in some areas, a duplication of facilities, may well bring about cross-code mergers. Whether this might eventually lead also to a single professional squad under the banner of a single team name in different competitions is another matter, but it's certainly possible. In many ways Harlequins are already doing it. And we can't rule out the possibility of further minor rule changes in both codes to facilitate this, perhaps on as well as off the pitch.

So rugby league continues to embrace change. That first great split with union in the George Hotel, Huddersfield, in 1895 created a professional sport. Over the years, rugby league has accepted its reliance on its spectators and general fan base. A hundred years into its history it accepted its essential relationship with television. Soon after union's own rule change in 1995, there were articles predicting that league would be re-absorbed into union within ten years. In the reality, league has gone from strength to strength, though both sports, of course, have grown both in extent and popularity throughout the period.

Rugby league gave me the opportunity to pursue a career as a professional sportsman and I remain grateful for that. It's a fast, open game whose object is to score tries, and that certainly suited me. It's a game that has always been able to identify its strengths and play to them.

Of course, an interesting question is what game I might have played if I'd started my career in 2009 rather than 1987. The answer, probably, given some of the player histories I've included in my *50 Of The Best*, is both! Undoubtedly I'd have my own manager, or agent, and my commitment to club or code would be limited to current contract terms. It's as simple as that.

Crossing codes, however, may become more difficult if demands on players in the different games continue to diverge. In many field positions, the two games now seem to demand a different body shape married to different physical attributes. Switching codes in the past has often involved switching position, and that's more likely to be the case in the future as Super League stresses speed and strength ever more, while union still retains the technicalities of line-out, ruck and maul, coupled with a scoring system that still favours the boot.

Within six years, however, both codes will have staged World Cup competitions in England. The development of either code will surely be influenced massively by the degree of success achieved in their respective competitions. Furthermore, I believe the development of rugby as a whole will hinge on their combined performances. I believe the two sports will increasingly cooperate while retaining their separate identities. And we are already in a new era. Australia no longer have what looked like a permanent hold on international rugby league honours. In union, after England's triumph in 2003, the southern hemisphere has reasserted its superiority, but this time in the shape of South Africa.

My *50 Of The Best* set out to be a retrospective celebration of rugby league's skills, its excitement and its spectacle. I focussed on the three decades that were host to my career in the sport and have described some of the game's great tries, great players and great stories. I loved scoring tries. That's what I did. It was my thing and I was pretty good at it, 501 times good at it! I hope that my collection of tries, players and stories has been an enjoyable read. I hope also that it's created a little more interest in rugby league – the fast, skilful, spectacular team game that I love.

I was the greatest try-scorer of my generation in a game that's about scoring tries. So, to finish my *50 Of The Best* I want to ask whether the days of the dedicated try-scorer might be over? Do the rigours of the modern game mean that there's no longer room for an out-and-out try-scorer? Maybe it's also harder to score tries now, because defences are so much better drilled. So we'll certainly know if another try machine is in our midst.